ROYAL MILE AND ARTHUR SEAT EDINBURGH

ROYAL MILE CASTLE ESPLANADE EDINBURGH

ATHELSTANEFORD EAST LOTHIAN
BIRTHPLACE OF THE SCOTTISH FLAG

The Scottish flag (Saltire) a white cross on a blue background is thought to be the oldest national flag in Europe and the Commonwealth. It was during a battle in 834 AD, King Angus believes that when seeing a cloud formation of a white saltire in the sky (which was the diagonal cross that St Andrew had been crucified on) was a sign from the saints, he proclaimed if the saints help them defeat the enemy he would make St Andrew patron saint of Scotland. On victory he made the Saltire the flag of Scotland in addition to St Andrew becoming the patron Saint of Scotland.

ROYAL MILE CASTLE HILL EDINBURGH

17	WELL	WITCHES WELL	CASTLE HILL	EDINBURGH
17	BUILDING	TARTAN WEAVING MILL	CASTLE HILL	EDINBURGH
17	SWORD	WILLIAM WALLACE	CASTLE HILL	EDINBURGH
18	BUILDING	CANONBALL HOUSE	CASTLE HILL	EDINBURGH
18	TELESCOPE	CAMERA OBCURA	CASTLE HILL	EDINBURGH
18	CANONBALL	CANONBALL HOUSE	CASTLE HILL	EDINBURGH
18	BUILDING	CASTLE HILL SCHOOL	CASTLE HILL	EDINBURGH
18	MUSEUM	WHISKY EXPERIENCE	CASTLE HILL	EDINBURGH
19	BUILDING	1st RAGGED SCHOOL	RAMSAY LANE	EDINBURGH
19	BUILDINGS	RAMSAY GARDEN, GOOSE PIE HOUSE	RAMSAY GARDEN	EDINBURGH
19	PLAQUE	RAMSAY GARDEN	RAMSAY GARDEN	EDINBURGH
19	WALL TABLET	RAMSAY LANE	RAMSAY LANE	EDINBURGH
19	WALL INSCRIPTION	MARRIAGE STONE	RAMSAY LANE	EDINBURGH
19	BUILDING	PALACE OF MARY OF GUISE	CASTLE HILL	EDINBURGH
20	CHURCH	THE HUB	CASTLE HILL	EDINBURGH
20	STEPS	CASTLE WYND NORTH	CASTLE HILL	EDINBURGH
20	STEPS	PATRICK GEDDES STEPS	JOHNSTONE TERRACE	EDINBURGH
20	CHAPEL	1st GAELIC CHAPEL	JOHNSTONE TERRACE	EDINBURGH
20	GARDENS	SCOTTISH WILDLIFE TRUST	JOHNSTONE TERRACE	EDINBURGH
20	CLOSE	SEMPLE'S CLOSE	CASTLE HILL	EDINBURGH
20	CLOSE	JOLLIE'S CLOSE	CASTLE HILL	EDINBURGH
20	CLOSE	SKINNER'S CLOSE	CASTLE HILL	EDINBURGH
20	COURT	BOSWELL'S COURT	CASTLE HILL	EDINBURGH

ROYAL MILE LAWNMARKET EDINBURGH

WE FIGHT NOT FOR GLORY, NOR FOR WEALTH, NOR HONOUR BUT ONLY AND ALONE
WE FIGHT FOR FREEDOM
WHICH NO GOOD MAN SURRENDERS BUT WITH HIS LIFE

FOR GOD AND ST ANDREW

ROBERT THE BRUCE
KING OF SCOTS
PLANTED HIS STANDARD
NEAR THE SPOT
WHEN THE
SCOTTISH PATRIOTS
UNDER HIS COMMAND
VANQUISHED THE ARMY OF
EDWARD II OF ENGLAND AT
THE BATTLE OF
BANNOCKBURN
24TH JUNE 1314

Robert the Bruce was born on 11 July 1274 and crowned King of Scotland on 25 March 1306 till his death 07 June 1329.

The Battle of Bannockburn was led by King Robert the Bruce of Scotland on the 24 June 1314. This was the moment that Scotland became an Independent Country. Scotland was independent for almost 400 years until 1 May 1707 when Scotland joined England in a political union to become Great Britain. There had previously been an informal agreement from 1603 when King James IV became the King of England and Ireland.

THOMAS THE RHYMER

Thomas was a poet and someone that could predict the future. His home was in Earlston in the Scottish Borders. The legend tells that Thomas fell asleep beneath a tree at the foot of the Eildon Hills. When he woke he saw the vision of a shining Lady on a Grey horse, this was the Queen of the Fairies and she entranced him and took him away to Fairyland. He remained there for what he thought had been three days, but was actually 7 years. When he left, the Queen gave him the gift of speaking the truth and told him many prophecies of great events in Scottish history.

One of the events he prophesied that there would be a bridge over the River Tweed which would be visible from the Eildon Tree. The Fairy Queen also told Thomas that she would return one day, so if you feel weary rest under the tree and you never can tell what will happen next. Thomas was a real person and lived in the 1200s and his rhymes have been popular for hundreds of years. His rhymers are the earliest examples of Scottish Poetry. Look in the Poetry Library of the Royal Mile for some examples. Stand by the stone and look for the Bridge or take a nap and see what happens.

ROYAL MILE	HIGH STREET	FROM NORTH AND SOUTH BRIDGE TO	CANONGATE	PAGE 3
41	CARVED ENTRY	PAISLEY CLOSE	HIGH STREET	EDINBURGH
41	OLD ST PAUL'S CHURCH	CARRUBBER'S CLOSE	HIGH STREET	EDINBURGH
41	GRASSMARKET CROSS	OLD ST PAUL'S CHURCH	JEFFREY STREET	EDINBURGH
41	PLAQUE	CARRUBBER'S CLOSE	HIGH STREET	EDINBURGH
41	ARCHBISHOP SPOTTISWOOD	CARRUBBER'S CLOSE	HIGH STREET	EDINBURGH
42	SIGN	SALTIRE SOCIETY	HIGH STREET	EDINBURGH
42	BUILDING	JOHN KNOX'S HOUSE	HIGH STREET	EDINBURGH
42	BUILDING	MOWBRAY HOUSE	HIGH STREET	EDINBURGH
42	CHURCH TRINITY APSE	CHURCH	CHALMER'S CLOSE	EDINBURGH
43	MUSEUM	MUSEUM OF CHILDHOOD	HIGH STREET	EDINBURGH
43	COURT	TWEEDDALE COURT	HIGH STREET	EDINBURGH
43	CHRISTIAN CENTRE	CARRUBBER'S CLOSE MISSION	HIGH STREET	EDINBURGH
43	WALL TABLET	N0. 2	ST MARY'S STREET	EDINBURGH
44	STORY TELLING CENTRE	ACCESS TO JOHN KNOX HOUSE	HIGH STREET	EDINBURGH
44	CARVED WALL TABLET	NETHERBOW GATE	HIGH STREET	EDINBURGH
44	WELLHEAD	NETHERBOW WELLHEAD	HIGH STREET	EDINBURGH
44	BELL	NETHERBOW BELL	HIGH STREET	EDINBURGH
44	BRASS COBBLES	NETHERBOW GATE OUTLINE	HIGH STREET	EDINBURGH

ISLANDS OF THE RIVER FORTH

FIDRA ISLAND

This is a volcanic island created around 335 million years ago. There is a lighthouse on the island which was built in 1885 by Robert Louis Stevenson's family, as were most lighthouses around the British shores. Robert Louis Stevenson often visited the beaches at Direlton the area known today as Yellowcraigs. Robert Lois Stevenson's inspiration for his novel Treasure Island came from his days looking at the Island.

LAMB ISLAND,

This Island is found between the islands of Fidra and Craigleith. The island was bought by Uri Geller in 2009 for the sum of £30,000 (He believes that it hides Egyptian Treasure).

These Islands are all close to North Berwick a small Town on the east coast a short distance from Edinburgh.

CRAIGLEITH ISLAND

This Island can be found close to North Berwick's harbour and its claim to fame was having the largest colony of Puffins in Britain numbering almost 30,000. It was also used in the breeding of rabbits for food.

BASS ROCK

The Bass Rock has more than 150,000 nesting Northern Gannets and is the largest single rock gannetry in the world. The naturalist David Attenborough called it the 12 wonder of the natural world.

North Berwick is a very beautiful Seaside town visited regularly by Robert Louis Stevenson. With golden sand beaches and plenty of things to do. Boat trips around the islands, 2 golf courses, the Sea Bird Centre, an outdoor sea swimming area which is free and safe for the children, great restaurants and fantastic coastal walks or climb the 600 foot Berwick Law (hill) which still has Bronze and Iron Age hut circles not to forget the World War 2 lookout post and the Napoleonic watch tower. A great day out for the family or stay a few days.

ROYAL MILE CANONGATE EDINBURGH FROM HIGH STREET TO CANONGATE KIRK

ROYAL MILE CANONGATE EDINBURGH		FROM CANONGATE KIRK TO ABBEY STRAND		
51	STATUE ROYAL POET	ROBERT FERGUSSON'S	CANONGATE	EDINBURGH
51	GRAVE	ROBERT FERGUSSON'S GRAVE	CANONGATE	EDINBURGH
51	CHURCH	CANONGATE KIRK	CANONGATE	EDINBURGH
51	CROSS	CANONGATE MERCAT CROSS	CANONGATE	EDINBURGH
52	CANONGATE KIRK	GRAVEYARD	CANONGATE	EDINBURGH
52	GRAVE	ROBERT FERGUSSON	CANONGATE	EDINBURGH
52	GRAVE	DAVID RICCIO	CANONGATE	EDINBURGH
52	GRAVE	AGNES MACALEES (CLARINDA)	CANONGATE	EDINBURGH
52	GRAVE	SIR WILLIAM FETTES	CANONGATE	EDINBURGH
52	GRAVE	ROBERT ADAM	CANONGATE	EDINBURGH
52	PAVING STONE	ROBERT ADAM	CANONGATE	EDINBURGH
53	CLOSE SIGN	DUNBAR'S CLOSE	CANONGATE	EDINBURGH
53	GARDENS	DUNBAR'S CLOSE GARDENS	CANONGATE	EDINBURGH
53	CLOSE SIGN	PANMURE CLOSE AND HOUSE	CANONGATE	EDINBURGH
53	PLAQUES	POPPY FACTORY ADAM SMITH	CANONGATE	EDINBURGH
53	CLOSE SIGN	CRIGHTON'S CLOSE	CANONGATE	EDINBURGH
53	LIBRARY	SCOTTISH POETRY LIBRARY	CANONGATE	EDINBURGH
54	PLAQUE	GOLFER'S LAND	CANONGATE	EDINBURGH
54	PLAQUE	GOLFER'S LAND	CANONGATE	EDINBURGH
54	WALL TABLET	GOLFER'S LAND	CANONGATE	EDINBURGH
54	WALL TABLET	84 CANONGATE	CANONGATE	EDINBURGH
54	BUILDING	82-84 CANONGATE	CANONGATE	EDINBURGH
54	WALL TABLET	JENNY HA'S	CANONGATE	EDINBURGH
54	PLAQUE	WHITEFORD HOUSE	CANONGATE	EDINBURGH
54	HOUSE	WHITEFORD HOUSE	CANONGATE	EDINBURGH
55	CLOSE	WHITE HORSE CLOSE	CANONGATE	EDINBURGH
55	PLAQUE WHITEHORSE CLOSE	WHITE HORSE TAVERN	CANONGATE	EDINBURGH
55	PLAQUE WHITEHORSE CLOSE	WILLIAM DICK	CANONGATE	EDINBURGH
55	COBBLES	IRON MAIDEN'S POSITION	CANONGATE	EDINBURGH
55	GUILLOTINE	IRON MAIDEN	CANONGATE	EDINBURGH
55	CITY GATE SIGN	WATERGATE	CANONGATE	EDINBURGH

NORTH BERWICK

North Berwick Law (Volcanic Core) 600 foot hill with magnificent views

Top of the Law, ancient housing and a Whale Bone stands for over 300 years

The Sea Bird Centre with boat trips around the islands to see puffins and seals.

Outdoor swimming and golden sands

Harbour and Marina

North Berwick the seaside town that Robert Louis Stevenson spent his summers. This once small fishing village is now a destination for holiday makers, with golden sands and coastal walks, boat trips, the sea bird centre, shops and restaurants all a short train journey from Edinburgh, fun for all.

ROYAL MILE ABBEY STRAND, HORSE WYND, ARTHUR SEAT AND QUEENS PARK AREA

CRAMOND ISLAND

This island is the only island that can be accessed at low tide by foot. The causeway runs at the foot of a row of concrete pylons constructed as a submarine defense during the Second World War. (Pictured below).

INCHKEITH ISLAND

As Inchgarvie, Inchkeith was used as a quarantine island in the 14th and 15th centuries. It was occupied by the English in the 16th century and Italian mercenaries fighting for the English in the 16th century. Mary of Guise renamed the island L'Île de Dieu (THIS ISLAND OF GOD). The soldiers also nicknamed it L'Île des Chevaux (THIS ISLAND OF HORSES).

CRAMOND ISLAND WHEN TIDE IS OUT

INCHCOLM ABBEY

INCHCOLM ISLAND. This Island may have been occupied since the 6th century when St Columba is said to have visited the priory. The Abbey has stood on the island since 1200. Danes are said to have buried their dead on the island by payment in gold to King Macbeth of Scotland and a tombstone of the 10th century stands as a memorial to the Danish leader.

THE 6 PARTS OF THE ROYAL MILE

EDINBURGH'S ROYAL MILE Starts at Edinburgh Castle and ends at Horse Wynd. It is believed to have been paved and cobbled from around the 1530s when James V had a duty charged for the use of the road.

CASTLEHILL Edinburgh is the short road that begins at the Castle Esplanade and ends at the Tolbooth Kirk. The gothic spire being the highest point in central Edinburgh constructed between 1842 and 1845, now the headquarters of the Edinburgh International Festival society. The other attractions in the street are the Camera Obscura & World of Illusions, (One of the oldest tourist attractions in the city), Canonball House, Witches Well, No.1 Ramsay Lane the first Ragged School, The Scottish Whisky Experience and The Scottish Weaving Mill previously the reservoir for Edinburgh.

THE LAWNMARKET Edinburgh is the street where the linen market was. Going down the hill on the left is the preserved 17th century townhouse Gladstone's Land. The south side has a strong Dutch influence. Lady Stair's House is where the Writer's Museum is, the High Court on the left with a Statue of David Hume Scottish philosopher, historian and economist outside. Directly opposite is the site of the last public hanging. See the plaque and cobbles. Do not miss Riddles Court and the first public library, and the notorious Deacon Brodie.

HIGH STREET, Edinburgh is between the Lawnmarket and the Canongate.
There are many interesting and famous places that can be seen. Parliament House, Charles II Statue, Heart of Midlothian, St Giles Cathedral, John Knox Statue and grave, Mercat Cross, Advocates Close, City Chambers, Real Mary Kings Close, Tron Kirk, Mowbray House, The Storytelling Centre, John Knox House, Festival Fringe Office,
The Trinity Apse Church and Museum of Childhood to list a few.

THE CANONGATE Edinburgh is named after the canons of Holyrood Abbey and the Scots word gait meaning "road". The Canongate is a small district at the heart of Edinburgh. The main street running through the area is called Canongate. The street forms the lower part of the Royal Mile Edinburgh's historic Old Town. Until formal incorporation into Edinburgh in 1856 the Canongate was a separate Burgh not part of Edinburgh. Look for the sites of The Girth Cross, Canongate Kirk and much more.

ABBEY STRAND Edinburgh is the small street leading up to the Palace gates. The brass letter S's in the cobbles that can be found across the start on the Abbey Strand were boundary markers of a sanctuary, which is five miles in circumference and takes in Holyrood Park. The Sanctuary was a safe place for people that were running away from creditors to live. The building that is now used as a gift shop was once homes for debtors.

HORSE WYND Edinburgh was the first part of the road to London and where the Royal Coaches started their journey south to London. The journey would take approximately 13 days. Opposite the Palace is the site of the new Scottish Parliament building, continue round and you will arrive in the Queens Park where Arthur Seat can be climbed on the Radical Road for a magnificent view of Edinburgh, Lothians and the Forth Bridges. Also take the road around the hill and see the Lochs and St Anthony's Chapel that stands above St Margaret's Loch on the hill.

THE NUMBERS RELATE TO THE PAGES THAT THE PICTURES AND INFORMATION ON THE PLACE OF INTEREST CAN BE FOUND

PURPLE WITH YELLOW NUMBERS ROYAL MILE BOOK 1 BLUE WITH YELLOW NUMBERS CITY CENTRE BOOK 2 RED WITH BLACK NUMBERS CITY CENTRE BOOK 2

CASTLE ESPLANADE EDINBURGH

Edinburgh Castle Esplanade is the area for four weeks of the year the world famous Edinburgh Military Tattoo his held. The month of August is the main show case of Edinburgh. This is when The Fringe Festival and Edinburgh International Festival takes place and tourists from around the world can be seen in their 100s of thousands. Looking around the Esplanade you can see memorials, statues and plaques to the regiments and heroes of the past battles. There is one obelisk one statue 3 plaques, 3 crosses, a wall fountain and the Ewart grave.

KING ROBERT THE BRUCE

EDINBURGH CASTLE DRAWBRIDGE

The drawbridge at the entrance to Edinburgh Castle with the statues of William Wallace and Robert the Bruce. Above the gateway, can be seen the coat of arms and motto of the Regiment of Scotland, who were based at Edinburgh Castle until the amalgamation of the Scottish regiments in 2006.

The motto "nemo me impune la cessit"
(no one attacks me with without punishment).

WILLIAM WALLACE

THE PLAQUE OF SIR WILLIAM ALEXANDER FIRST BARON OF NOVA SCOTIA

In 1621, King James granted Sir William Alexander the land in North America between New England and Newfoundland, as Nova Scotia ("New Scotland"). To promote the settlement of Nova Scotia, the Baronetage of Nova Scotia was created in 1624. Scots Law, baronets had to "take sasine" by symbolically receiving the earth and stone of the land of which they were baronet. To make this possible, as Nova Scotia was so far away, the King declared that sasine could be taken either in Nova Scotia or, "at the Castle of Edinburgh as the most eminent and principal place of Scotland".

91ST PRINCESS LOUISE'S ARGYLLSHIRE HIGHLANDERS

PRINCESS LOUISE Her Royal Highness, Marchioness of Lorne, 9th Duchess of Argyll and Queen Victoria's daughter. She had many honours bestowed upon her. The 91st Argyllshire Regiment name changed in her honour to 91st (Princess Louise's Argyllshire Highlanders) Regiment of Foot. She had a strong connection with Canada and a province (Alberta), a mountain (Alberta) and villages of Caroline and Alberta named after her. The inscription on the memorial Drinking Fountain above the trough reads;
THE PRINCESS LOUISE'S ARGYLLSHIRE HIGHLANDERS.

THE KING'S OWN SCOTTISH BORDERERS

THE KING'S OWN SCOTTISH BORDERERS On the 19th March 1689 David Leslie Earl of Leven gathered a regiment of soldiers within two hours to defend the City of Edinburgh. For Leven's regiment's gallantry in defending Edinburgh and later at the Battle of Killiecrankie with a resounding victory for the Jacobites lead by James VII of Scotland and II of England, the magistrates of Edinburgh gave the unique right of recruiting by the beat of the drum, marching through the Edinburgh streets with drums beating and flags flying and bayonets fixed. The regiment was later named The King's Own Scottish Borderers.

FREDERICK DUKE OF YORK

FIELD MARSHAL HIS ROYAL HIGHNESS FREDERICK DUKE OF YORK (1763-1827) was appointed Commander in Chief of the British Army in 1795. His parents King George III and his mother Queen Charlotte were instrumental in shaping Edinburgh's New Town with streets named by and after them. King George III was the first King of Great Britain and Ireland.

KING GEORGE III (George William Frederick) was born 4 June 1738 in London. He became king in October 1760 at 22. His wife was Charlotte and they had 16 children, 10 sons and 6 daughters and were married for 57 years. He died in January 1820 at 81. During his reign he had Edinburgh's new town built and purchased Buckingham House in London in 1762 which later became Buckingham Palace.

GORDON HIGHLANDERS MEMORIAL

GORDON HIGHLANDERS
The memorial is to the officers and men of the Gordon Highlanders who lost their lives in the South African war from 1899 to 1902 in Natal, Transvaal, Cape Colony and The Orange Free State.
The Gordon Highlanders was an army infantry regiment from 1881 until 1994.
The regiment took its name from the Clan Gordon and recruited principally from Aberdeen and the North-East of Scotland.

RUNIC CROSS
78th HIGHLAND REGIMENT

The Runic Cross was erected in 1862 for the memory of the officers, non-commissioned officers and private soldiers of the 78 highland regiment who died at the suppression of the First Relief of Lucknow in 1857 during the Indian Mutiny (1857-59). Eight men of the 78th Highland Regiment were awarded the Victoria Cross and the regiment also received the Victoria Cross during the campaign. The troubles started due to the bullets being covered with pig fat which they had to bite. Putting pork of any kind in their mouths is against the religious beliefs of Hindus and Muslims.

SCOTTISH HORSE
MEMORIAL CROSS

The above monument is a memorial to the Scottish Horse Regiment who were killed during the South African War of 1901-2

COLONEL MACKENZIE
92ND HIGHLANDERS

The Celtic cross above was erected in memory of Colonel Kenneth Douglas Mackenzie a member of the 92nd Highlanders for forty two years.
He died on duty in 1873.

72ND HIGHLANDERS
OBELISK MEMORIAL

72ND HIGHLANDERS
The Obelisk was erected in memory of the officers, Non-commissioned officers and men of the Duke of Albany's 72nd highlanders who died in Afghan campaigns in 1878, 1879 and 1880.

PRESENT GUN

PREVIOUS GUN

LOOK UP AT CALTON HILL ABOUT 7 MINUTES BEFORE ONE O'CLOCK AND SEE THE BALL GO UP THE MAST

The Nelson Monument is a commemorative tower in honour of Vice Admiral Nelson, situated on top of Calton Hill Edinburgh. The Time Ball was added in 1852 as a time signal to shipping in Leith harbour and the Forth estuary. The Time Ball is raised just before 1pm each day (not Sunday), and at precisely 1pm is released to descend the mast which gives the visible sign to the ships that it is one O'clock. Nelsons Monument Edinburgh was originally linked to a master clock in the City Observatory.
The One O' Clock Gun was installed on the ramparts at Edinburgh Castle in 1861 to provide an audible signal, when the weather was bad and the Time Ball was not visible to the ships in Leith and on the River Forth. The Time Ball was linked to the One O' Clock Gun (in 1861) by a wire that stretched across from the Nelson Monument to Edinburgh Castle. The Time Ball and the One O'clock gun are now linked electronically.

The present and previous One O'clock Guns.
The present gun looks out over Princes Street and the previous gun can be seen overlooking the harbour in Dunbar East Lothian.

SERGEANT CHARLES EWART, Battle of Waterloo 18th June 1815. In 1938 the actual remains of Ensign Ewart were reinterred on Edinburgh Castle's Esplanade. (Pictured) battle date, the eagle standard of the French Army and memorial stone. Look behind the memorial stone and you can see his head stone.

THE TAKING OF THE FLAG

As Ewart fought his way deep into the heart of the 45th French Infantry, he was caught in a fierce fight with a French officer. The French officer was saved from Ewart's fatal strike by the arrival of his senior officer, Francis Kinchant. The French officer surrender to Kinchant saving his life. No sooner had Ewart turned away from the scene when he heard a gunshot just behind him. When he turned back, he saw senior officer Kinchant fall of his horse and the French Officer trying to hide his gun with which he had just killed Kinchant. Ewart, furious at what the French Officer had done, he lashed out with his sword ignoring the Frenchman's pleas for mercy and took the Frenchmen's head off with one stroke of his sword. (See the sword in Edinburgh Castle) Ewart was now near to the 45th French Infantry standard bearer. Rather than retreating, Ewart continued forward and battled through to take the flag back to his own lines and into history.

"The Fight for the Standard at the Battle of Waterloo" by Richard Ansdell R.A.

The painting depicts Ensign Ewart at The Battle of Waterloo with the French standard. This painting can be seen in Edinburgh Castle.

ROYAL SCOTS DRAGOONS

In Ewart's own words, what was to follow ;

"It was in the first charge I took the eagle from the enemy. I had a hard contest for it, he made a thrust at my groin, I parried it off and cut him down through the head. After this a lancer came at me; I threw the lance off by my right side and cut him through the chin and upward through the teeth. Next, a foot-soldier fired at me and charged me with his bayonet, which I also had the good luck to parry, and then I cut him down through the head; thus ended the contest. As I was about to follow my regiment, the general said, 'My brave fellow, take that to the rear; you have done enough till you get quit of it', which I was obliged to do, but with great reluctance. I retired to a height, and stood there for upwards of an hour, which gave a general view of the field, but I cannot express the horrors I beheld. The bodies of my brave comrades were lying so thick upon the field that it was scarcely possible to pass, and horses innumerable. I took the eagle into Brussels amid the acclamations of thousands of spectators who saw it. Displayed in the Regimental Museum in Edinburgh Castle is the sword said to have been used at Waterloo by Ensign Charles Ewart.

ROYAL MILE CASTLEHILL EDINBURGH

CASTLEHILL, Edinburgh the short road that begins at the Castle Esplanade and ends at the Tollbooth Kirk (THE HUB). The gothic spire being the highest point in central Edinburgh constructed between 1842 and 1845, now the headquarters of the Edinburgh International Festival society and on the opposite side of the street the Camera Obscura & World of Illusions which is one of the oldest tourist attractions in the city of Edinburgh. You can also see Canon Ball House, Witches Well, Ramsay Garden, The Scottish Whisky Experience and the Weaving Mill.

THE WITCHES WELL

The Witches Well, found in a corner on the wall of the Scottish Weaving Mill.

WITCHES WELL Edinburgh (pictured)
This site, situated at the top of Castlehill on the west wall of The Tartan Weaving Mill is where an iron wall fountain commemorates the place where over three hundred women were burned at the stake, accused of being witches in the 16th Century. There were more Witch burnings carried out at Castlehill than anywhere else in Europe.

TARTAN WEAVING MILL CASTLEHILL EDINBURGH

This is an opportunity to see the full story of kilt making, from the wool on the sheep via the weaving of the tartan cloth to the making of the kilt. Try out the weaving loom for yourself, or dress up in ancient Scottish costume for a souvenir photograph. The picture on the left shows the Tartan Weaving Mill from Ramsay Garden, below a sword that would have been used at the time of William Wallace.

A reservoir was first built on this site as early as 1675. This was later demolished in 1849 to make way for the present structure The Tartan Weaving Mill.

Replica sword outside the weaving mill that William Wallace may have used.

CANONBALL HOUSE

TOP OF CANONBALL HOUSE

THE CANONBALL

The cannonball embedded in the wall can be seen from the steps that go down to Johnstone Terrace from Castlehill. Legend has it that in 1745 the castle garrison fired the cannon ball at Bonnie Prince Charlie's encampment at Dunsapie Loch but missed and hit the house.

CANONBALL HOUSE can you spot the canon ball embedded in the wall. The story is that the canon ball was carefully placed here by engineers to mark the height above sea-level of the fresh springs which provided Edinburgh with its first piped supply of fresh water, in about 1621. The cannon ball can be seen embedded in the wall above the first-floor window in Castle Wynd North. On the opposite side where the Tartan Weaving Mill is now, was the site of a reservoir that served the well heads in the old town of Edinburgh. In 1991 the reservoir was no longer required and is now conserved as the Edinburgh Tartan Weaving Mill.

THE CAMERA OBSCURA & WORLD OF ILLUSION

THE CAMERA OBSCURA (Outlook tower) and World of Illusion Edinburgh. This was one of the original tourist attractions in 1850s Edinburgh, the first attraction being the Walter Scott Monument. The Camera Obscura gives an amazing live panoramic view of the city of Edinburgh. See the people in Edinburgh walking about the streets below and pick them up in your hand. The telescopes let you view amazing rooftop views of the city. It was named the Outlook Tower in 1892. Take a walk around the outside walkway at the top of the Tower for more amazing views.

CASTLEHILL SCHOOL EDINBURGH / THE SCOTTISH WHISKY EXPERIENCE

Castle hill Primary School opened in 1889 and is now closed as a school. The front of the school can be seen from Johnston Terrace Edinburgh. It now houses The Scottish Whisky Experience which is entered from the Castlehill across from Ramsay Lane.

SCOTTISH WHISKY EXPERIENCE

The Scottish Whisky Experience tells the story of the history of whisky making, from the stills in the hills to the world wide industry of today. See possibly the world's largest collection of Scotch whisky and the chance to taste the nectar of Scotland. The whisky experts will help you find the ideal whiskies for your individual taste in the McIntyre whisky gallery. There is also a chance to shop for the whisky you love. No driving afterwards.
(Tasting over 18 years of age only).

FIRST RAGGED SCHOOL IN SCOTLAND

THE SCULPTURED BIBLE ABOVE THE DOOR

The bible above the door is inscribed with the words "search the scriptures" "ST JOHN V S V 39"
Ramsay Lane was the site of the first Ragged School in Scotland founded by Dr Thomas Guthrie in 1847. Ragged Schools were free education for the poor and homeless children. There is a Ragged School museum in London.

RAMSAY GARDEN Ramsay Lodge was where Allan Ramsay the poet lived in the 1700s. Later it was developed into 16 houses for student accommodation with a magnificent view of the New Town Edinburgh. They are now private residence. The Ramsay Garden houses are a prominent feature of Edinburgh with their red ashlars and white exteriors and were first built by Alan Ramsay in 1733. Can you see the cat on the hot tin roof?

The arrow shows Allan Ramsay's original Goose pie octagonal shaped house.

WEDDING STONE Walking down Ramsay Lane towards the Mound. A stone built into the wall can be seen. This is a marriage stone where the two sets of initials of the betrothed and the date of the marriage were set in stone on the walls of their home. An old Scottish custom.

PALACE AND CHAPEL OF MARY OF GUISE
The first building you will walk past on the Castehill is the site where Mary of Guise had her Palace (pictured).
Mary of Guise was the daughter of Antoinette of Bourbon and Claud Count of Guise. Mary of Guise married King James V in 1538. They had a daughter born in Linlithgow Palace in 1542 and at a week old became the Queen of Scotland on her father's death. Her name was Mary. (Mary Queen of Scots). The building was also used as the Scottish Parliament in 1990s.

THE HUB stands at the foot of Castlehill. The Hub's spire is the highest point in central Edinburgh. The building was constructed around 1845 as the Victoria Hall to house the General Assembly of the Church of Scotland. In 1929 the Church of Scotland ceased to use the building and it became a temporary home for a variety of congregations. It was named the Highland Tolbooth and then St John's Church in 1956 and finally closed in the early part of the 1980s. In 1999 the building was transformed into The Hub, offices and a performance space for the Edinburgh International Festival.

On the wall of Johnston Terrace above where the first Gaelic Chapel was established is a sign that reads

EAGLAIS
GHAIDHEALACH
DHUN – EIDEANN
SITE OF THE FIRST
GAELIC CHAPEL
1769

Take a walk down the Castle Wynd South steps and the gate on the right is entry to a Scottish Wildlife Trust Garden and the Chapel site.

PATRICK GEDDES STEPS

CASTLE WYND NORTH STEPS

CASTLE WYND NORTH STEPS

CASTLE WYND NORTH STEPS The picture of the steps shown above right is taken from Johnston Terrace looking up to the Castlehill and the entrance to the Castle esplanade. Look for the cannonball in the wall of Canon Ball House on the right.

CASTLE WYND SOUTH STEPS The picture on the left is looking up the steps from the Grassmarket to Johnstone Terrace. (**PATRICK GEDDES STEPS**)

CLOSE'S OF CASTLEHILL

BOSWELL'S COURT is the site of the famous Witchery Restaurant and Lodging.

SKINNER'S CLOSE original site of Fortunes tavern before moving to Nicholson Square and then St Andrew's Square.

JOLLIE'S CLOSE Land and building at the top of the close owned by Patrick Jollie, and later by Alexander Jollie who was a writer in 1859. Now part of the Witchery hotel apartments.

SEMPLE'S CLOSE was the entrance to the mansion of Lord Semple (SEMPILL) Commander of the Black Watch and Major of the Cameronians. The mansion was purchased by him in 1743 but was originally built for Lady Semple in 1638.

ROYAL MILE LAWNMARKET EDINBURGH

When walking down the Lawnmarket Edinburgh you will pass many openings called closes or entries. These are the access to the houses and courtyards that people lived in from the 1100's. The council of Edinburgh, looking to attract successful merchants (wealthy Businessmen) to the City of Edinburgh and offered them a strip of land called a toft, with a condition that they had to build a house on the land within one year and one day. Over the centuries the tofts were divided into two parts Forelands and Backlands. In the 1500s due to the noisy and dirty conditions of the streets the best houses were built on the backlands which were accessed by openings called closes or entry's. The forelands were accessed and looked onto the streets where the livestock were kept. This was one of the reasons for the bad smells.

VICTORIA TERRACE VICTORIA STREET AND WEST BOW

The foot of Castle hill you will find the steps at the Upper Bow leading down to Victoria Street, West Bow and the Grassmarket or continue down the Royal Mile into the Lawnmarket where you will find closes, courts and entry's to search.

UPPER BOW STEPS

JAMES'S COURT 493 -495 LAWNMARKET EDINBURGH

Named after the builder James Brownhill James's Court was built around 1725.
The philosopher David Hume and James Boswell the lawyer and author lived here. The court was destroyed by fire and re-built in 1857.

MYLNE'S COURT 513 LAWNMARKET EDINBURGH

The first open court of its type in Edinburgh, it was built in 1692 by Robert Mylne master mason to the King. The buildings were renovated in 1914, becoming Edinburgh University Halls of Residence.

FISHER'S CLOSE LAWNMARKET

BRODIE'S CLOSE LAWNMARKET

*** RIDDLES COURT LAWNMARKET**

JAMES'S COURT LAWNMARKET

WEST ENTRY

MID ENTRY

EAST ENTRY LAWNMARKET

**** MYLNE'S COURT LAWNMARKET**

LADY STAIR'S CLOSE LAWNMARKET

WARDROP'S CLOSE LAWNMARKET

When walking down the Royal Mile you will come across a number of close's courts and entrys where the spelling of the names of the place are different; Milne's / **Mylne's,** Riddles / Riddell's they are all the same place. The owners of the properties called the area after themselves as the wealthy did in these days.

RIDDLE'S (RIDDELL'S) CLOSE AND COURT. The merchant Baillie John McMorran built a house for himself in 1590. He was one of the wealthiest residents of Edinburgh at that time. Inside you can see the different interiors from the 16th - 19th centuries. The story of the building can be seen in the painted ceilings by Patrick Geddes. See where the banquet was held when King James the sixth stayed here with his Queen.

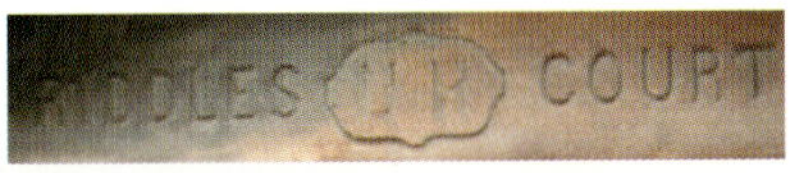

SCOTTISH CENTRAL LIBRARY 312-320 Lawnmarket founded by Carnegie UK Trust in 1921 and opened in 1953 after renovations. It was later merged with the National Library of Scotland in 1974. This was part of Fisher's Land the building built for Thomas Fisher a merchant in 1699.

GLADSTONE'S LAND LAWNMARKET Edinburgh. Halfway down the Lawnmarket section of the Royal Mile you can experience what life was like in the Old Town by visiting Gladstone's Land. This is a restored tenement building to show the conditions people lived in, in Edinburgh in the 17th Century. Also visit Lady Stair's House the Writer's Museum and Makers' Court.

WILLIAM (DEACON) BRODIE (28 September 1741 – 1 October 1788), more commonly known as Deacon Brodie lived in Brodie's Close in the Lawnmarket Edinburgh, where he also had his workshop. William Brodie was a Scottish cabinet maker and Deacon of trades (This is where the name Deacon came from). By day, William Brodie was a respectable tradesman, a Deacon and a member of the Edinburgh Town Council. When evening came he used his skills as a burglar. The money from his crimes was used to maintain his second life, including five children, two mistresses and a gambling habit. He was also a member of the Edinburgh Cape Club founded in the 1700s. The main meeting place was the Isle of Man Arms in Craig's Close in the Old Town of Edinburgh. A meeting place for the wealthy and nobility where all manor of frivolities would take place. When Deacon Brodie was eventually caught for trying to rob the Royal Mint, he was arrested and sentenced to hang. In 1788 he was taken to the Edinburgh Tolbooth (jail) and hanged by the neck. The Tolbooth is no longer there but is marked with brass cobbles and the Heart of Midlothian. Deacon Brodie's life inspired Robert Louis Stevenson to write the strange case of Dr Jekyll and Mr Hyde. William Brodie designed and erected the gallows in the High Street and was also the first to hang on them. The Gallows are marked with a plaque and cobbles at the corner of George IV Bridge across from David Hume's Statue.

A PLASTER MANEQUIN OF DEACON BRODIE

THE ISLE OF MAN ARMS

DEACON BRODIE'S GRAVE

LAWNMARKET ENTRY TO LADY STAIR'S CLOSE

ROBERT BURNS LIVED HERE

LADY STAIRS CLOSE

LADY STAIR'S CLOSE
MANSION OF LADY STAIR
RESTORED BY 5TH EARL OF ROSEBERY
ONLY RELIC OF CLOSE WHERE
IN TAVERN OF 1717
SIR RICHARD STEEL GAVE SUPPER TO
COMPANY OF ECCENTRIC BEGGARS

Writers' Museum is housed in Lady Stair's House which was built in 1662. This was originally called Lady Gray's Close the widow of Lord William Gray who was the wealthiest merchant of the time. After his death the house was sold to the Earl of Stair and the house was renamed after his wife on his death Lady Stair's House. The Writer's Museum is dedicated to the lives and work of Scotland's great literary figures. Rare collections include early editions, manuscripts, portraits, photographs, and personal belongings of Robert Burns, Sir Walter Scott and Robert Louis Stevenson.

MAKERS' COURT & CLOSE

LADY STAIR'S HOUSE

MAKARS' COURT is the area outside Lady Stair's House, The Writer's Museum. Look beneath your feet and find the words of the great people Like Robert Fergusson, Walter Scott and Robert Burns. Makars' Close from the Mound and two of the paving stone that can be seen in Makars' Court and the steps to Makars' Court Lady Stair's House the Writer's Museum.

SEE ALL THE SLABS IN MAKARS' COURT IN THE CITY BROCHURE (pages 61, 62, 63)

THE LAWNMARKET WELLHEAD

The Lawnmarket Wellhead can be found up from St Giles Cathedral at the junction of the Lawnmarket and the High Street. This is where the residents would collect their fresh drinking water every day.

THE LAWNMARKET WELLHEAD

THIS WELLHEAD OR CISTERN, WAS BUILT IN 1835. IT PROBABLY REPLACED A CISTERN OF AROUND 1675, REMOVED WHEN GEORGE IV BRIDGE WAS BUILT.

THE CISTERNS PROVIDED WATER FROM COMISTON SPRINGS VIA THE CASTLEHILL RESERVOIR FOR THE INHABITANTS OF THE OLD TOWN. THEY BECAME IMPORTANT MEETING PLACES WHERE LONG QUEUES FORMED. THEY FELL INTO DISUSE IN THE 19TH CENTURY WHEN SUPPLIES TO INDIVIDUAL HOUSES BECAME POSSIBLE.

THIS WELLHEAD WAS REPAIRED AND RESTORED BY THE EDINBURGH OLD TOWN RENEWAL TRUST AND LOTHIAN AND EDINBURGH ENTERPRISE LIMITED IN 1997.

DAVID HUME was born on the 26 April 1711 in Edinburgh, he was a Scottish philosopher and historian. He was one of the most important figures in the history of Western philosophy and the Scottish Enlightenment. David Hume attended the University of Edinburgh. Hume achieved great literary fame as a historian when publishing The History of England.

David Hume lived from 1771 until his death in 1776 at his home in St. Andrew Square in Edinburgh's New Town. The actual site of his home is 21 St David Street. There are two thoughts on how St David's Street was named firstly after King David I son of Malcolm III and the other after David Hume.

(Picture taken 2013)

LOTHIAN CHAMBERS GEORGE IV BRIDGE ENTRANCE

LOTHIAN CHAMBERS EDINBURGH

The Lothian Chambers Building was built in 1904 and was used for the administration of Midlothian Council. The building is now used as a venue for marriages. On the corner of the building at the Lawnmarket is a plaque showing the place where the last person in Edinburgh was hanged. A man in his early 30's battered and slit the throat of a 23 year old girl in a crime of passion. The brass cobbles in the street show where the gallows were.

LOTHIAN CHAMBERS ENTRANCE WEST PARLIAMENT SQUARE

LAST PUBLIC EXECUTION

The plaque and cobbles show the place where the gallows stood and the site of the last man to hang in public in Edinburgh.

EDINBURGH'S LAST PUBLIC EXECUTION

The site of the gallows is marked by the three brass plates set at the edge of the pavement. Near to the site of the Edinburgh Tolbooth. George Bryce the Ratho murderer was executed her on the 21st June 1864 the last public execution in Edinburgh. The first public execution from the same gallows was on 1 October 1788, a William (Deacon) Brodie. The gallows the same William (Deacon) Brodie had designed and funded the year before.

ROYAL MILE - HIGH STREET - EDINBURGH

When walking up and down the High Street Edinburgh you will pass many openings called closes or entry. These are the access to the houses that people lived in from the 1100s. The council of Edinburgh, looking to attract successful merchants (wealthy businessmen) to the City of Edinburgh, offered a strip of land called a toft with a condition that they had to build a house on the land within one year. Over the centuries the tofts were divided into two parts Forelands and Backlands. In the 1500s due to the noisy and dirty conditions of the street the best houses were built on the Backlands which were accessed by openings called closes or entry. The merchants not only lived in the houses but also worked, kept live stock and grew there own vegetables. The Forelands were accessed by and looked onto the street where the live stock was kept. Below are the High Street Closes and Entry's you can see today. Pictured below are the signs of the closes and entry's from the crossroads at St Mary's Street, Jeffrey Street, Canongate and the High Street Edinburgh.

WORLD'S END CLOSE

TWEEDDALE COURT

BARON MAULE'S CLOSE

NORTH GRAY'S CLOSE

MORRISON'S CLOSE

 # CARRUBER'S CLOSE #

HYNDFORD'S CLOSE

BAILIE FYFE'S CLOSE

PAISLEY CLOSE

CHALMERS' CLOSE

BISHOP'S CLOSE

MONTEITH'S CLOSE

TRUNK'S CLOSE

HOPES COURT

SOUTH GRAY'S CLOSE

TODDRICK'S WYND

FOUNTAIN CLOSE

DICKSON'S CLOSE

CANT'S CLOSE

MELROSE CLOSE

CROSS THE JUNCTION AT NORTH AND SOUTH BRIDGE EDINBURGH

LYON'S CLOSE

STEVENLAW'S CLOSE

NEW ASSEMBLY CLOSE

FLESHMARKET CLOSE

JACKSON'S CLOSE

BURNET'S CLOSE

NORTH FOULIS' CLOSE

COVENANT CLOSE

ANCHOR CLOSE

OLD STAMP OFFICE CLOSE

OLD ASSEMBLY CLOSE

GEDDES' ENTRY

BORTHWICK'S CLOSE

OLD FISHMARKET CLOSE

WARRISTON'S CLOSE / WRITER'S COURT

BELL'S WYND

ROXBURGH'S CLOSE

ADVOCATE'S CLOSE

BYRE'S CLOS

ROYAL MILE HIGH STREET EDINBURGH

HIGH KIRK OF EDINBURGH, ST GILES CATHEDRAL

There are records that show a parish church being in Edinburgh in 854 A.D. The parish church of Edinburgh was formally dedicated by the bishop of St Andrews on 6 October 1243. The parish church of Edinburgh was subsequently deconsecrated and named in honour of the patron saint of Edinburgh, St Giles.

ST GILES was a Greek holy man who settled in the south of France in the 7th century and was said to be associated with the early Frankish Kings, in particular Charles Martel (688–741). St Giles is seen in the carving above the west door of St Giles Cathedral Edinburgh (pictured below). St Giles is said to have stopped a hunter's arrow with his hand and saved a deer. There are many stories of St Giles and his miracles throughout history. St Giles later became the patron saint of both Edinburgh and the Cathedral now known as St Giles Cathedral. St Giles died on the 1st September 721 A.D.

ST GILES SAVING THE DEER

BISHOP FORBES **ALEXANDER HENDERSON**

BISHOP WILLIAM FORBES. In 1634 William Forbes became the first bishop of Edinburgh, with St Giles as his Cathedral. Bishop Forbes Died on the 12 April 1634 shortly after becoming the first bishop of Edinburgh. Bishop William Forbes is buried in St Giles Cathedral.

ALEXANDER HENDERSON a Presbyterian minister moved from his parish in Leuchars, St Andrews to become the minister of the High Kirk of St Giles in Edinburgh. When King Charles visited Scotland in 1641 Alexander Henderson was appointed Dean of the Chapel Royal at Holyrood. He was also instrumental in the writing of the National Covenant and became the Moderator of the general assembly on more than one occasion. He died in Edinburgh in 1646 and is buried in Greyfriar's Churchyard Edinburgh.

ROBERT THE BRUCE **JAMES I OF SCOTLAND** **JAMES VI OF SCOTLAND**

ROBERT THE BRUCE (King Robert I)

Robert I, known as Robert the Bruce, became King of Scots on 25 March 1306. At the Battle of Bannockburn in June 1314, he led a Scottish army and defeated the English army lead by Edward II. To confirm an independent Scottish monarchy in 1320 a letter was sent to Pope John XXII declaring that Robert the Bruce was their rightful monarch. This letter was the 'Declaration of Arbroath' and it asserted the antiquity of the Scottish people and their monarchy. In 1324 Robert the Bruce received papal recognition as king of an independent Scotland. Robert died on 7 June 1329. He was buried in Dunfermline Abbey and his heart is buried in Melrose Abbey.

JAMES I

James I became King on the death of his father in 1406 but he was not crowned at Scone Palace until 1423.
The reason for the 17 years delay in his being crowned was that he was imprisoned in London. While in prison his uncle Robert of Albany ruled Scotland and was happy for James to remain in prison hoping that one day he or his son Murdoch would become king. When James was released at age 30 he took over as king. He then began restoring the monarchy and forfeited the lands of the rebellious nobles including the Dukes of Albany. He was a strong leader and introduced social and economic legislation and founded the Scottish Court of Session. In 1437 James was killed in a Dominican Monastery in Perth.

JAMES VI of SCOTLAND AND I OF ENGLAND

James son of Mary Queen of Scots and Henry Darnley, was born in Edinburgh Castle in 1566. James became the youngest King of Scotland at the age of thirteen months. In 1603, he also became king of England and Ireland. He continued to reign in all three kingdoms for 22 years. In 1605 a small group of Catholics, led by a man called Robert Catesby, devised a scheme to kill James and as many members of Parliament as possible. Catesby's plan involved blowing up the Houses of Parliament on 5th November as in the Guy Fawkes rhyme, Remember Remember the 5th of November gunpowder treason and plot, Catesby being Guy Fawkes. The 5th of November was chosen because James was due to open Parliament on that day. At 57 years and 246 days, his reign in Scotland was the longest of any previous King. James died in 1625 at the age of 58 and is buried in Westminster Abbey.

ST ANDREW

When visiting St Giles Cathedral take a walk round the exterior and see the many carvings. High above the east door of St Giles Cathedral stands a carved statue of St Andrew holding two fish. Below the statue an angel holds a scroll with his name carved on it and above two angels hold a shield with the cross of St Andrew. You will also see a number of other carvings above and around the doorway which dates from the late 1380s. You will find shields with the crosses of St George and St Andrew, and decoration of Thistles, Roses and Fleurs de Lis. Also shields with coats of arms that include James VII and Queen Anne.

GAVIN DOUGLAS was born in 1474 at Tantallon Castle, Dunbar East Lothian. Gavin Douglas was a Scottish Bishop, royal court poet, courtier and translator. Gavin Douglas was appointed provost of St. Giles Church, Edinburgh, around 1501 and is best known for his translation of Virgil's Aeneid into Scots, the English language of the lowlands of Scotland. He was made bishop of Dunkled in 1516 and died in London in 1522.

JOHN KNOX was born in the Haddington area of East Lothian in approximately 1514 he was appointed minister of the Church of St. Giles in 1560. John Knox was married twice and his second marriage in 1564 was not looked upon favourably because John Knox was 50 and his new wife was only 17. He was considered to be the greatest Reformer in the history of Scotland. Knox died on 24 November 1572 in Edinburgh his epitaph "Here lyeth a man who in his life never feared the face of man, who hath been often threatened with dagger, but yet hath ended his dayes in peace and honour."

GAVIN DOUGLAS **JOHN KNOX**

ALEXANDER I **DAVID I** **ALEXANDER III**

ALEXANDER I was born in 1078 and was the eldest brother of three David I and Alexander III his brothers. Alexander I established an Augustinian priory at Scone sometime between 1114 and 1122. In 1123 Alexander I on a journey had to shelter on Inchcolm Island in the Firth of Forth during a storm, he promised to build a monastery in thanks for being saved from the storm but died in 1124 before being able to keep his promise. His brother David I kept his brothers promise and invited Augustinian canons to establish a priory on the island and it later became an Abbey in 1235. Alexander I died in Stirling on the 23 April 1124 and is buried in Dunfermline Abbey.

DAVID I King David I was born in 1084, he spent many years in the court of Henry I, which gave him a good education. David became King of Scotland in 1124 on the death of his brother. He established the feudal system in Scotland. He also introduced many novel ideas such as silver coinage and promoting education. He also carried on his brother's quest to build many Abbeys which included Holyrood Abbey and Inchcolm Abbey. David died peacefully in Carlisle in 1153 at the age of 69 and is buried in Dunfermline Abbey. During his reign he founded The Abbey of Holyrood in 1128 and built the Chapel in Edinburgh Castle a memorial to his mother Queen Margaret who died in 1093. Later becoming Saint Margaret in 1250.

ALEXANDER III Alexander was born on the 4 September 1241. He was King at the age of 7 from 1249. At 21 he formally approached the Norwegian King Haakon for the Western Isles which Haakon rejected. In 1263 King Haakon died and his successor agreed to the Treaty of Perth by which he gave the Isle of Man and the Western Isles to Scotland in return for a large sum of money. Norway kept control of Orkney and Shetland. Alexander died when he fell from his horse in Kinghorn in Fife on 18 March 1286. Travelling on his way from Edinburgh to visit his Queen on her birthday, which was the next day. In 1886, a monument to Alexander III was erected at the approximate location of his death in Kinghorn. Alexander was buried in Dunfermline Abbey in 1286.

JOHN KNOX BURIAL PLACE The small stone above the 23 marks the position of John Knox grave, in the Graveyard of St Giles Cathedral. (Now a council car park). John Knox was a very important part of the history of the church in Scotland and was behind the Government in 1560 severing contact with the Pope and catholic faith. He was the head of the Scottish reformation and from 1559 till his death in 1572 was the minister of the High Kirk of St Giles, in Edinburgh.

ADAM SMITH 1723 – 1790 lived in Panmure House in Lochend Close in the Canongate and is buried in the Canongate Kirk Graveyard, behind the Canongate Kirk. Adam Smith was a Scottish moral philosopher and a pioneer of political economy. He was one of the key figures of the Scottish Enlightenment. In 1776 The Wealth of Nations, is considered his magnum opus and the first modern work of economics. Smith is cited as the father of modern economics. In 2009 Adam Smith was named among the "Greatest Scots" of all time, in a vote run by Scottish television.

The location of the Edinburgh Mercat Cross between 1617 and 1756 can be seen in an octagonal arrangement of cobble stones on the pavement outside the entrance to Old Fishmarket Close in the High street Edinburgh. This was the second position in which the Mercat Cross had stood, the first being in the centre of the road further down the High Street.

5th DUKE OF BUCCLEUCH

The statue of Walter Francis Montagu Douglas Scott (1806 – 1884) the 5th Duke of Buccleuch and the 7th Duke of Queensbury was erected in West Parliament Square Edinburgh High Street in 1888. The Duke of Buccleuch was born in Dalkeith House Midlothian and was a very wealthy land baron. He became the Duke on the death of his father at the age of 13. He was knighted in 1835 and served in Prime Minister Peel's government in the 1840s. There is still a Duke of Buccleuch to this day, the 10th Duke of Buccleuch and the 12th Duke of Queensbury lives in Drumlanrig Castle. He is also the Chief of Clan Scott. Drumlanrig Castle is home to the world renowned Buccleuch Art collection.
The Castle and Estate can be found south of Sanquhar in Dumfriesshire off the A76.

THE ORIGINS OF WHISKY Alcohol has been around since the Egyptians were building the Pyramids, giving the workers beer and bread to help them through the hot days. Wine has also been known to be in existence for up to 10,000 years through religious scripts. It is not known when Whisky was first made but records of distillation are shown from the 11th century. The first written record of whisky was in 1494. The name whisky originally from the Gaelic "Uisge Beatha", meaning 'water of life'. In 1644 the Scottish Government imposed a tax on whisky and in 1707 after the union of Scotland and England a malt tax was introduced on the 23 June 1725 which caused riots over Scotland, this indirectly increased the cost of making whisky, as malt is the main ingredient. In 1824 George Smith the originator of the Glenlivit whisky was the first to gain a legal licence to distil whisky when the English government introduced a law to legalize the production of whisky. The oldest bottlers of whisky are Cadenhead's who have been bottling whisky since 1824.
Whisky and all alcoholic drinks are restricted to persons of over 18 years and should not be consumed by anyone younger.

HAGGIS THE SCOTTISH NATIONAL DISH

Haggis is known worldwide as the national dish of Scotland. A hairy beast that runs the heather covered hills of the highlands. The dish is in fact a combination of sheep's innards, oatmeal and spices, all wrapped up in a sheep's stomach.
Originally it was a meal for the poor using the leftovers of the sheep and cooking it in the skin of the stomach. In 1786 Robert Burns wrote the ode to a Haggis which immortalised the haggis as a delicacy greater than any other cuisine. Due to Robert Burns popularity, Haggis also became very popular. After the death of Robert Burns his friends met annually on his birthday the 25 January to celebrate his life, which is how the tradition of the Burns Supper started. To this day on the 25 January worldwide Burns Suppers take place with the Haggis being honoured with the ode Burns wrote in 1786.

ADDRESS TO A HAGGIS BY ROBERT BURNS

Fair fa' your honest, sonsie face,
Great chieftain o' the puddin'-race!
Aboon them a' ye tak yer place,
Painch, tripe, or thairm:
Weel are ye wordy o' a grace
As lang's my airm.

The groaning trencher there ye fill,
Your hurdies like a distant hill,
Your pin wad help to mend a mill
In time o need,
While thro your pores the dews distil
Like amber bead.

His knife see rustic Labour dicht,
An cut you up wi ready slicht,
Trenching your gushing entrails bricht,
Like onie ditch;
And then, Oh what a glorious sicht,
Warm-reekin, rich!

Then, horn for horn, they stretch an strive:
Deil tak the hindmaist, on they drive,
Till a' their weel-swall'd kytes belyve
Are bent like drums;
Then auld Guidman, maist like to rive,
'Bethankit' hums.

Is there that ower his French ragout,
Or olio that wad staw a sow,
Or fricassee wad mak her spew
Wi perfect scunner,
Looks down wi' sneering, scornfu view
On sic a dinner?

Poor devil! see him ower his trash,
As feckless as a wither'd rash,
His spindle shank a guid whip-lash,
His nieve a nit:
Thro bloody flood or field to dash,
Oh how unfit!

But mark the Rustic, haggis-fed,
The trembling earth resounds his tread,
Clap in his wallie nieve a blade,
He'll make it whissle;
An legs an arms, an heads will sned,
Like taps o thrissle.

Ye Pow'rs, wha mak mankind your care,
And dish them out their bill o fare,
Auld Scotland wants nae skinking ware
That jaups in luggies:
But, if Ye wish her gratefu prayer,
Gie her a Haggis!

A TRADITIONAL HAGGIS

The traditional Haggis main course is;
Haggis, Neeps and Tatties.

When you buy a haggis preferably from a good butcher it is already cooked and all that is required of you is to heat it up in a saucepan, oven or microwave. Neeps (turnip) and Tatties (potatoes) are peeled, cut up and boiled in water in a saucepan. When cooked drain water, mash and season and served on a plate with the Haggis.

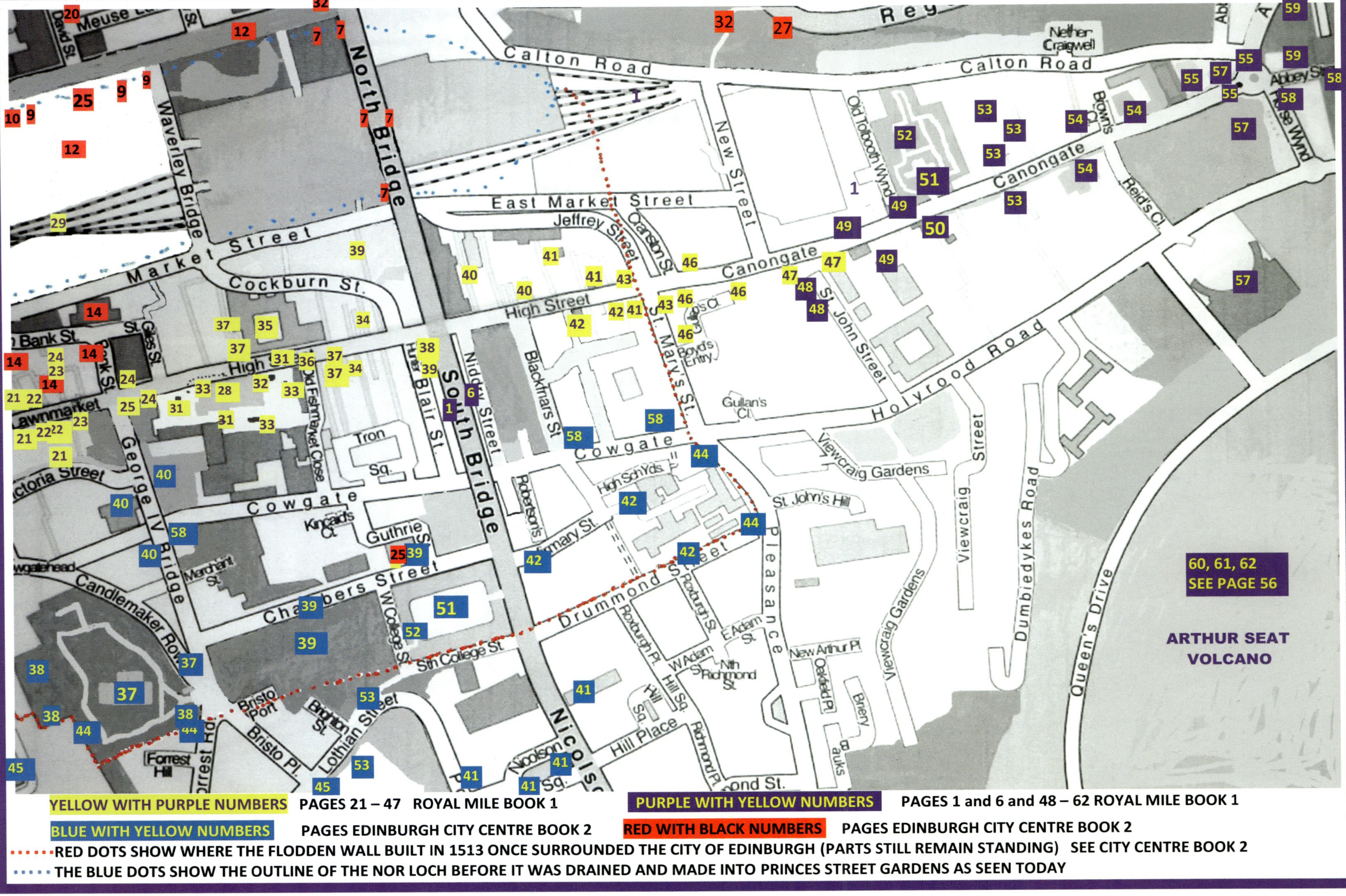

YELLOW WITH PURPLE NUMBERS PAGES 21 – 47 ROYAL MILE BOOK 1

PURPLE WITH YELLOW NUMBERS PAGES 1 and 6 and 48 – 62 ROYAL MILE BOOK 1

BLUE WITH YELLOW NUMBERS PAGES EDINBURGH CITY CENTRE BOOK 2

RED WITH BLACK NUMBERS PAGES EDINBURGH CITY CENTRE BOOK 2

RED DOTS SHOW WHERE THE FLODDEN WALL BUILT IN 1513 ONCE SURROUNDED THE CITY OF EDINBURGH (PARTS STILL REMAIN STANDING) SEE CITY CENTRE BOOK 2

THE BLUE DOTS SHOW THE OUTLINE OF THE NOR LOCH BEFORE IT WAS DRAINED AND MADE INTO PRINCES STREET GARDENS AS SEEN TODAY

KING CHARLES II Edinburgh

(May 1630 –Feb 1685) King Charles II Statue dressed as a Roman Emperor on horseback is the oldest lead cast statue in Great Britain. The statue of King Charles II stands in Parliament Square behind St Giles Cathedral and was first erected in 1685.

EXCHEQUER BUILDING
IN PARLIAMENT SQUARE EDINBURGH

The Exchequer Building in Parliament Square was erected in 1685. The Bank of Scotland used offices in the building in 1695 when the bank was incorporated by royal charter.
One year after the incorporation of the Bank of England in Thread Needle Street London.

HEART OF MIDLOTHIAN

The Heart of Midlothian is a heart-shaped mosaic built into the pavement next to St Giles on the High Street. Together with brass markers set into the pavement, it records the position of the 15th-century Old Tolbooth demolished in 1817, which was the administrative centre of the town, the prison and one of several sites of public execution. Some people spit on the heart. Although it is now said to be done for good luck, it was originally done as a sign of disdain for the former prison.

THE BRASS COBBLES SHOWING
THE OUTLINE OF THE EDINBURGH TOOLBOOTH

JAMES BRAIDWOOD 1800 – 1861

The father of the British Fire Service, James Braidwood was born in Edinburgh and founded the world's first municipal fire service in Edinburgh in 1824. A statue of James Braidwood can be seen in Parliament Square and is dedicated to his memory. He was a pioneer of the scientific approach to fire-fighting, an approach that has saved lives all over the world.

MERCAT CROSS EDINBURGH was first mentioned in 1365 when the cross stood in the middle of the High Street. In 1885 the cross was placed on a new octagonal drum substructure at its current location. The use of a Mercat Cross in Scotland was for important civic announcements. In Edinburgh government proclamations that affected all of Scotland were also publicly read at the cross, for example, announcements concerning successions to the monarchy and the calling to parliament. The only Mercat Cross that remains in its original form and position can be found in Prestonpans East Lothian.

The Unicorn is the ancient emblem of Scotland and stands at the top of the Mercat Cross. The coats of arms that surround the Mercat Cross are shown Below. Prestonpans Mercat Cross is pictured Left.

THE MEDALLIONS THAT ARE ON THE MERCAT CROSS IN PARLIAMENT SQUARE

LEITH COAT OF ARMS

EDINBURGH COAT OF ARMS

CANONGATE COAT OF ARMS

ROYAL COAT OF ARMS OF BRITAIN

SCOTTISH COAT OF ARMS

UNIVERSITY OF EDINBURGH COAT OF ARMS

ENGLISH COAT OF ARMS

IRISH COAT-OF-ARMS

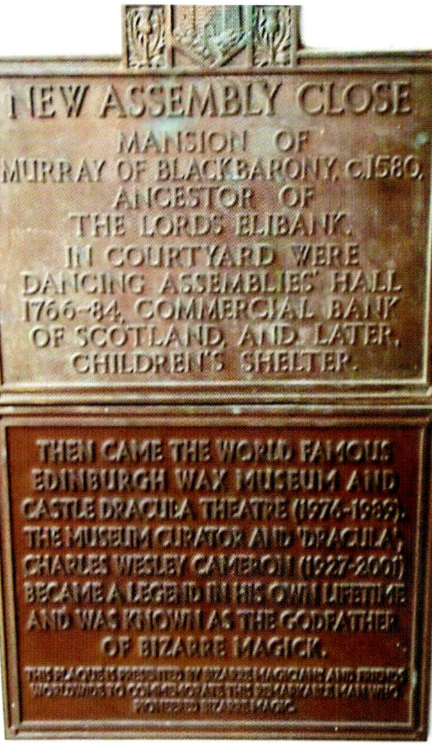

NEW ASSEMBLY CLOSE in around 1580 was the site of the mansion of Murray of Blackbarony. It was also where the commercial Bank of Scotland was housed from 1766 – 1784 and The Edinburgh Waxworks Museum from 1976 - 1989.

OLD ASSEMBLY CLOSE was the dance hall of the 1700s. The founder of the University of Edinburgh Library, Clement Little lived here as did his brother William Little who was Lord Provost of Edinburgh in 1591. Scene of the great fire of 1824 when the fire spread from the Tron to Parliament Square.

OLD STAMP OFFICE CLOSE HIGH STREET EDINBURGH

The Close's in Edinburgh were named after the owners of buildings in the close at the time and thus had many names through time. Old Samp Office Close was where the Stamp Office was for many years until it moved to Waterloo Place in 1821. It was the first place the Royal Bank of Scotland had offices and where Countess Eglinton and her seven beautiful daughters lived. Lady Eglinton and her daughters were the people to invite to any dance or party in the 1700s. There was also a school where the famous Flora McDonald of Skye was educated. She was Famous for assisting Bonnie Prince Charlie in his escape after the battle of Culloden. The close has also been named after 2 taverns Ship Tavern close and Fortune's Close.

ADVOCATES CLOSE was named after Lord Advocate Sir James Stewart of Goodtrees. The Stewart family owned and lived in the Close from 1648 – 1769. Advocates Close has had many names as the name would change by the owner at the time.

THE ACCESS TO THE TWO CLOSE'S BELOW WERE CLOSED IN 1932 CRAIG'S CLOSE

There were two parts to Craig's Close
High Street – Cockburn Street (closed) and Cockburn Street – Market Street which is still open. Craig's Close was the site of The Isle of Man Arms. The Edinburgh Cape Club's main meeting place.

ALLAN'S CLOSE was removed when the City Chambers extended their premises but a part of Allan's Close remains underground and can only be seen on the Real Mary King's Close tour of the old streets of Edinburgh.

EDINBURGH CITY CHAMBER

THE CITY CHAMBERS FORMERLY, THE ROYAL EXCHANGE designed by John Adam. This building was erected 1753 – 1761 to be used as an exchange and customs house. In 1811 it became the City Chambers when the Town Council moved here from the Tolbooth. Extended in 1904 and 1934 it has served as the administrative centre for Edinburgh Corporation and since 1975 for the Council of the City of Edinburgh.

THE FIRST POLICE FORCE IN THE UK

ALEXANDER THE GREAT WITH HIS HORSE BUCEPHALUS

Cast in Bronze in 1883 the wondrous horse Bucephalus the horse that Alexander the Great rode for thousands of miles and through many battles to create his mighty empire. Both Horse Bucephalus and owner Alexander the Great stand in the square of Edinburgh City Chambers on the High Street in the Royal Mile.

THE HIGH CONSTABLES OF EDINBURGH

In 1611 the privy council of King James VI ordered the Burgh to appoint constables to impose law and order on the streets of Edinburgh. This was taken over by a regular police force in Edinburgh in 1805.

HUGH MILLER There is a bust of Hugh Miller in the Hall of Heroes at the Wallace Monument in Stirling. Hugh Miller was editor of Witness, an evangelical newspaper established in 1840 by the Scottish geologist and writer. He committed suicide in December 1856. A shocked Western world mourned him, and his funeral procession was among the largest in the memory of Edinburgh residents.

IAN RANKIN

PROFESSOR PETER HIGGS **DAME ELIZABETH BLACKADDER**

46664 **RICHARD DEMARCO**

GEORGE KERR

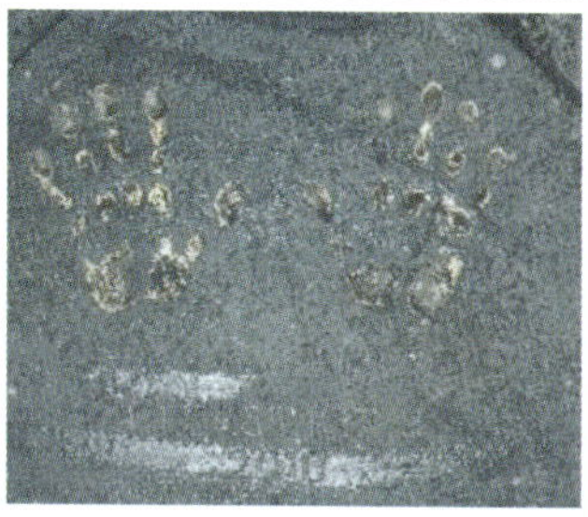

J K ROWLING

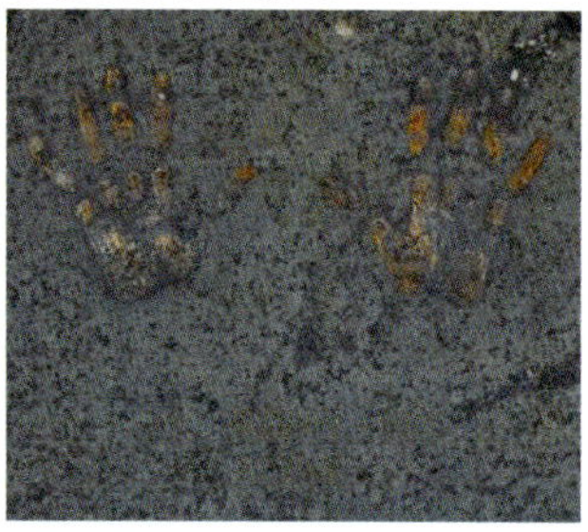

SIR CHRIS HOY

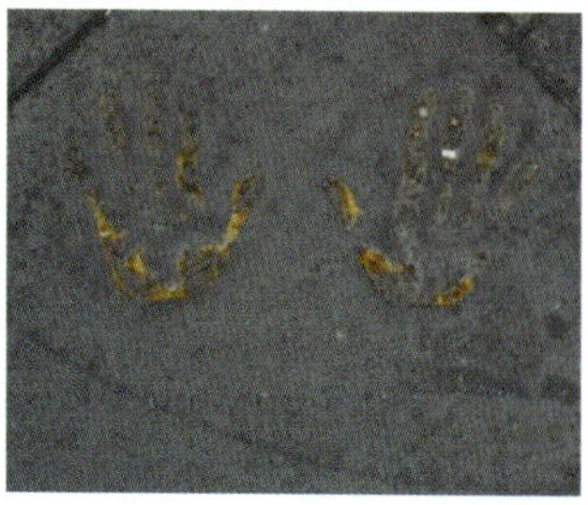

STEVEN AGED 14
LIVING WITH HIV

IT'S IN OUR HANDS

ANNIE LENNOX

HOLLYWOOD IN EDINBURGH In the paving stones of the City Chambers quadrangle you can see the golden hands of famous people awarded by Edinburgh, such as Author J.K. Rowling Olympic champion cyclist Sir Chris Hoy, Artist Richard Demarco, Author Ian Rankin, Singer Annie Lennox, Scientist Professor Peter Higgs,
George Kerr CBE Judo 10th Dan, Dame Elizabeth Blackadder Painter, 46664 Concert Nelson Mandela speech.
These pictures were taken in 2014 before Tom Gilzean icon of the Royal Mile still raising funds for charity now in his 90s was honoured.

ANCHOR CLOSE was named after a tavern that was at the top of the close in 1714, this was a meeting place of the Crochallan Fencibles, a club with a number of the most distinguished men of the city. The Crochallan Fencibles Club was founded by William Smellie, a printer who founded the Encyclopaedia Britannica. He also printed the first Edinburgh edition of Burns in 1787. On the east side of the Close there are two 17th-century buildings, originally of four storeys. A doorway on the west side of the Close has a 17th-century inscription:

LORD BE MERCIFUL TO ME.

JAMES GILLESPIE was an Edinburgh city merchant and founder of James Gillespie's Hospital and School. The hospital opened in 1802 and could accommodate up to 66 Pensioners and the school.
The school was originally sited at Gillespie Crescent near to the original hospital at Wright's house. James Gillespie was born in Edinburgh on the 28 April 1726 and died at his home in Spylaw, Colinton a suburb of Edinburgh on 8 April 1797. His brothers, John and James were Tobacco and snuff merchants at 231 High street Edinburgh and had their own factory at the back of their house at Spylaw. Due to the civil war in the Americas they were a main British supplier to the trade and controlled the prices at the time.

THE REAL MARY KING'S CLOSE This is a real look back in to Edinburgh's past. The underground streets and places where the people of Edinburgh lived, a historically accurate example of life in Edinburgh between the sixteenth and nineteenth centuries, Tales of ghosts, legends and murders. Where the plague victims were walled up and left to die. Take the guided tour based on a one time resident, and listen to the fascinating stories. Writer's court leading to Warriston close and Real Mary Kings Close Edinburgh and the entrance to the under ground streets.

WARRISTON'S CLOSE

REAL MARY KING'S CLOSE

JOHN KNOX MANSE

The site of John Knox's Manse can be found in Warriston's Close. Go in towards The Real Mary King's Close and turn left and down steps and you will see the plaque next to a black door.

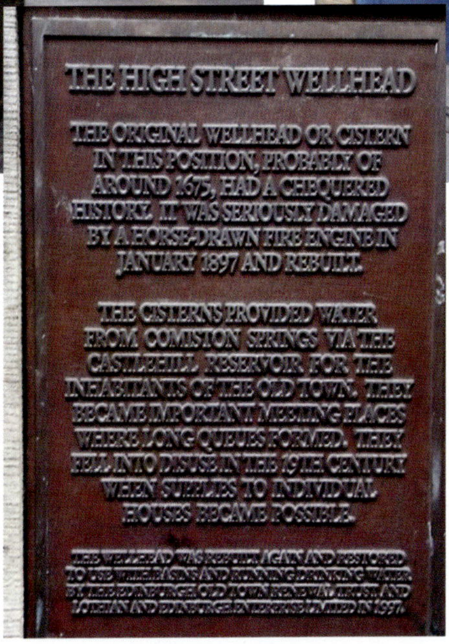

THE HIGH STREET WELLHEAD

can be found up from the Tron Kirk in the High Street Edinburgh. The Wellheads (cisterns) provided water for the residents of Edinburgh in the 1600s. This Wellhead is one of four that can still be seen in Edinburgh the others are in the Lawnmarket, Netherbow and the Grassmarket.

LOTHIAN & BORDERS POLICE INFORMATION CENTRE & MUSEUM

This is the place for people to report crime get directions and information on all aspects of the Police force and their duties. There is also an exhibition of the history of The Police in Edinburgh the criminals like William (Deacon) Brodie the raffles of his time. Burke and Hare the serial Killers for money.

LOOKING DOWN THE HIGH STREET TO THE TRON CHURCH

THE TRON FROM THE NORTH BRIDGE

THE TRON KIRK EDINBURGH looking down the High Street during the Edinburgh Festival in August with the Tron Kirk in the distance. The Tron Kirk was built in the 17th century and closed as a church in 1952.The area around the Tron was the original place for bringing in the bells (celebrating the changing of the old year to new). The Tron is now an indoor market and free fringe venue.

THE BLACK TURNPIKE. MARY QUEEN OF SCOTLAND'S LAST NIGHT IN EDINBURGH 1567

The Black Turnpike, also known as the 'Auld Bishop of Dunkeld's Lodging' was built in 1461 on the south side of the High Street immediately west of where the Tron Kirk now stands. It was demolished in 1788 to make way for Hunter Square and Blair Street. The plaque below can be seen on the wall of the City Chambers. The inscription reads "On this site stood the lodging of Sir Simon Preston of Craigmillar (known as the Black Turnpike) the lord provost of the city of Edinburgh 1566 – 1567 in which lodging Mary Queen of Scotland after her surrender to the confederate lords at Carberry Hill was imprisoned over night in Edinburgh 15 June 1567 in a stone chamber 13 foot square and 8 foot high. On the following evening she was conveyed to holyrood and thereafter to Loch Leven Castle as a state prisoner. After 19 years of captivity, Mary was tried and condemned to death in October 1586, ending only with her execution at Fotheringhay on 8 February 1587".

AT THE TRON

HUNTER SQUARE SIR CHRIS HOY

Sir Chris Hoy MBE, won his first Olympic gold medal in 2004. He won 3 Olympic gold medals in Beijing and was knighted by the queen in 2009. In the London Olympics of 2012 all British gold medal winners also received a post box painted gold in their home city/town. Sir Chris Hoy won 2 gold medals and there are 2 post boxes in Edinburgh (pictured left) in Hunter Square of the Royal Mile and in Hanover Street across from the Art Galleries at the foot of The Mound. Sir Chris Hoy is Scotland's most successful Olympian. Sir Chris Hoy was educated at George Watson and Edinburgh University. With 6 Olympic gold medals and 11 world championships he is most definitely a world sports superstar.

FIND YOUR TARTAN

DEFINITION OF TARTAN from the Scottish Register of Tartans Act (2008) Section 2:

Section 2: A tartan is a design which is capable of being woven, consisting of two or more alternating coloured stripes Which combine vertically and horizontally to form a repeated chequered pattern. The tartan pattern is traditionally known as the sett of the tartan. Below are a number of examples of Scottish Tartans and 2 American, which can be found on the Scottish register of tartans. Pop in to The Edinburgh Clothing Company at 93 South Bridge Edinburgh to see if you can find your Clan Tartan or see www.tartanregister.gov.uk for all tartans registered in the Scottish tartans register a comprehensive list is also available on www.thesotlandkiltcompany.co.uk/clan-shop.

CAMPBELL

JOHN MUIR WAY

CAMERON ANCIENT

MUNRO

MACDONALD

GORDON

SIKH

FLOWER OF SCOTLAND

MARSHALL

SOUTH CAROLINA

NORTH CAROLINA

UNIVERSITY OF EDINBURGH

Originally Tartan was normal everyday clothing which was made locally to the area you lived. Tartan was seen by the English as a form of uniform, an Act of parliament band the wearing of tartan in 1747, this was the Act of Proscription. This came about due to the Jacobite uprising which ended at the Battle of Culloden 1746. The Act of Proscription was ended by George III in 1782 which allowed highland dress to be worn again after 35 years being outlawed.
There are 34 US States with their own tartan.

Creator of All About Edinburgh

My name is Gary Marshall and I was born and have lived in Edinburgh for over 50 years. All About Edinburgh brochures first came to me when on holiday in Paris France. When my wife and I were looking for the site of the Bastille. We seemed to be going round in circles and finally, finding someone to ask who would speak English, I asked where the site of the Bastille the famous Jail from the revelotion was? He pointed and said there. We looked into the middle of a roundabout (which we had been round twice) to see a pillar covered in posters, this was the historic site of the jail, The Bastille. I then thought that it must be the same worldwide when visiting places, not knowing what you are actually standing beside or walking past. Over the next 6 years I have put together the 3 All About Edinburgh booklets. It has been a great learning curve and I now know more about my own city than I had in the previous 50 years. I hope you are enjoying this booklet as much as I have when compilling it, and hope you will also enjoy the other two parts of the trilogy. More info can be found on www.allaboutedinburgh.co.uk

On 10 November 1861 a building that had stood for 250 years sunk into the ground (107 High Street Edinburgh) burying the residents of the building. 35 were found dead and on clearing the rubble the rescuers heard a voice from beneath the collapsed building.

"Heave awa lads I'm no deid yet".

The rescuers pulled the boy (Joseph McIver) to safety and the town had the sculpture placed above the new named close in his memory, with the inscription which has been modified to read.

"HEAVE AWA CHAPS I'M NO DEAD YET"

PLAQUE BELOW THE CROSS

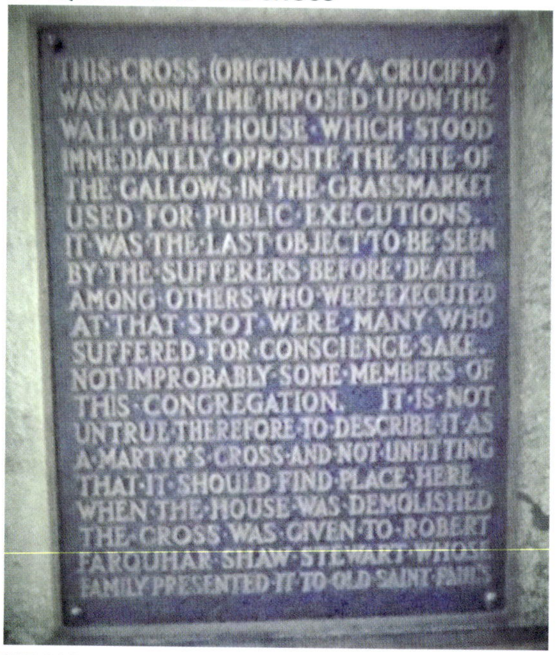

OLD ST PAULS CURRUBBER'S CLOSE

GRASSMARKET CROSS

OLD ST PAULS JEFFREY STREET

CARRUBBER'S CLOSE

THE HOUSE OF ARCHBISHOP SPOTTISWOOD

OLD ST PAUL'S CHURCH

St Giles Cathedral, became the Cathedral of Edinburgh in 1634 and the last bishop at St Giles, Alexander Rose, left the Cathedral in 1689 taking with him most of his congregation. He founded a new place of worship in an old wool store in Carrubber's Close which lies close to the present site of Old St Paul's. Old St Paul's Chapel also contains the Martyrs' Cross, a small iron cross that originally hung in the Grassmarket opposite the gallows, and was the last object seen by condemned criminals before execution.

ARCHBISHOP JOHN SPOTTISWOOD lived in a town house in Carrubber's Close High Street Edinburgh in 1578. John Spottiswood on 18 June 1633 officiated at Charles I Scottish coronation in the Canongate kirk.
He was one of the most powerful men of his time. Charles I made him President of the Exchequer. The day after his death his History of the Church and State of Scotland, was presented to Charles I by John Maxwell, the bishop of Ross. The Archbishop's magnum opus was not published until 1655.

THE SALTIRE SOCIETY was founded in 1936 and its purpose is to improve the quality of life in Scotland and make people around the world see the values Scotland has to offer everyone in every walk of life. The Saltire Society has no political affiliation and anyone is welcome to become a member.

FÀILTE is Gaelic for welcome.

TRINITY APSE CHALMER'S CLOSE

TRINITY APSE can be found at the foot of Chalmers Close. This is the only surviving area of the Trinity College Church founded in 1460 which was moved brick by brick from its original site where the Waverley Station is now. Inside are the Pictish standing stones and medieval church brasses. Also a shortcut to Jeffrey Street Edinburgh and the Waverley Rail Station

Hopes Court is hidden in the corner between John Knox House and Mowbray House. A door-way with a carved lintel still remains. A drawing can be found in the Society of Antiquities Scotland.

GEORGE JAMESON born in Aberbeen in the late 1500s was recognised as the best portrait painter of his time from the British Isles. He live in Mowbray House and died in 1644 in Edinburgh and is buried in Greyfriar's Churchyard. His work can be seen in the National Gallery of Scotland on the Mound.

JOHN KNOX HOUSE & MOWBRAY (MOUBRAY) HOUSE

JOHN KNOX HOUSE

The house John Knox lived in can be found at the Netherbow in the High Street Edinburgh next to Mowbray House (pictured). This is one of the oldest buildings in Edinburgh built in the 1470s. John Knox was born in 1510 and was a Scottish clergyman and leader of the Protestant Reformation and was also considered the founder of the Presbyterian denomination. There is a statue of John Knox in the inner quadrangle of the Assembly Hall on the Mound. He also had a house in Warriston's Close and his grave is in the car park No.23 at the back of St Giles Cathedral.

MUSEUM OF CHILDHOOD

MUSEUM OF CHILDHOOD

The world's first museum to be dedicated solely to the history of childhood was opened in 1955. The museum of Childhood contains five galleries with toys and games, both contemporary and antique, from around the world.

CARRUBBER'S CHRISTIAN CENTRE

CARRUBBER'S CLOSE MISSION is a non-denominational Evangelical church in the High Street Edinburgh. The Atheist Meeting House was founded in 1858 in Carrubber's Close to be found a few yards up the High Street towards the Castle. The American Evangelist D. L .Moody came to Edinburgh and was successful in raising funds to open the present mission hall in 1883.
To this day Carrubber's Christian Mission continues to have strong trans-Atlantic links.

TWEEDDALE COURT 14 High Street Edinburgh.
This Court was named after John Tweeddale 1st Marquess of Tweeddale. Built in 1576 and then purchased in early 1600s by the Earl of Lothian for his daughter which she then gifted to her grandson in 1645. The British Linen Company occupied Tweeddale Court in 1791 till 1807. A grizzly murder also took place in Tweeddale Court in 1806, when William Begbie a porter of the British Linen Company was stabbed through the heart and robbed of thousands of bank notes he was carrying from a branch at the top of Leith. A major amount of notes were later recovered but the murderer was never caught. It is suspected that the murderer was later caught for another bank robbery of a similar description in Glasgow, but it was never proven. The thief was tried for the Glasgow robbery and found guilty, imprisoned and later died in Old Calton Jail in Regent Road.

EDINBURGH CITY IMPROVEMENT ACT OF 1867

The streets of Edinburgh were engulfed in fire in 1824 which destroyed around 20 tenements and left 8 dead and over 400 homeless. At the same time, the population of Edinburgh was doubling from 80000 to 160000. The growth was due to immigration into the poorer areas of the city from the rural areas of Scotland and also Irish immigrants due to the Irish potato famine. Edinburgh required major housing development and the first building erected was at 2 St Mary's Street, Edinburgh.

The houses with outside landings face to the back of the buildings with entry from a close or narrow passageway from the main street. A good example of this is in Dunbar Close pictured above with the gardens to the back. The first tenements built in the Lawnmarket were up to 7 stories high and access to each door was off an internal narrow winding staircase. No elevators or lifts in these flats. There are also many courtyards from James Court in the Lawnmarket to White Horse Close in the Canongate. Each close, court or entry hides something different so go in and explore.

THE SCOTTISH STORY TELLING CENTRE AT THE NETHERBOW PORT

The Scottish Story Telling Centre allows access to John Knox House, the oldest house in Edinburgh, the Netherbow Theatre, and is the headquarters of the Scottish Storytelling Network. The Storytelling Court is open to the public, and has an exhibition for children. There is a book shop , gift shop and Licensed Café for all to use.

STORY TELLING CENTRE

NETHERBOW PORT

BRASS COBBLES NETHERBOW GATE

NETHERBOW PORT

When the Canongate was a Burgh of its own, there were walls around the city of Edinburgh with gates known as Ports. The Story Telling Centre, combined with John Knox House was just a short distance from the historic main gateway of Edinburgh. The gateway, the Netherbow Port, was rebuilt many times. The great bell being hung originally in 1621 and can be seen at the top of the bell tower above the main entrance of the Story Telling Centre. The Netherbow Port was the most important gateway as it stood halfway down the Royal Mile. The port access to and from the Canongate which was at that time a separate Burgh. The walls were built originally for defence against invading armies into Edinburgh in the 1500s after the battle of Flodden. In the 1700s the demolition of sections of the wall began. The Netherbow Port was pulled down in 1764, and demolition continued into the 19th century. Today, a number of sections of the three successive walls survive, although none of the ports remain. You can see and find out more about Edinburgh's history in the Museum of Edinburgh in the Canongate.

THE NETHERBOW BELL 1621

NETHERBOW WELL

CRINGLETIE HOUSE HOTEL

This 4 star rated Hotel is the ultimate place for your weekend away or your Wedding. We cater for all types of occasions and have activities from Highland Games, Shooting, Fishing, Golf and Horse Riding and much more......... We also have a private cottage with outdoor Jacuzzi with amazing views and walks.

"the only Visit Scotland 4 Gold Star Hotel in the Borders".

www.cringletie.com Tel 01721 725750 email enquires@crngletie.com
Cringletie House Hotel on the A703 Edinburgh Road Peebles EH45 8PL

ROYAL MILE - CANONGATE - EDINBURGH

THE CANONGATE, Edinburgh is named after the canons of Holyrood Abbey and the Scots word gait meaning "road". The Canongate was an independent Burgh (area) outside the walls of Edinburgh. Now as one of 6 parts of the Royal Mile.
The Canongate starts at St Mary's Street and ends at the junction of Horse Wynd and Abbey Strand. Until formal incorporation into Edinburgh in 1856 Canongate was a separate burgh. There is a circular marker in the cobbles on the south side of the road. This is where The Cross of St John at one time stood and was the original boundary of the Canongate. (no longer there).There is also a plaque on the wall with information about the cross. There were 2 further crosses in the Canongate, one stood outside the Tolbooth (The Mercat Cross) which now stands in the Canongate Kirk and the other stood at the foot of the Canongate where a further circle of cobbles shows where The Girth Cross stood. Only one seems to have survived.

SOUTH SIDE OF CANONGATE FROM ST MARY'S STREET

GULLAN'S CLOSE CANONGATE

GIBB'S CLOSE CANONGATE

PIRRIE'S CLOSE CANONGATE

CHESSEL'S COURT CANONGATE

OLD PLAYHOUSE CLOSE CANONGATE

SUGAR HOUSE CLOSE CANONGATE

BAKEHOUSE CLOSE CANONGATE

WILSON'S COURT CANONGATE

COOPER'S CLOSE CANONGATE

CRIGHTON'S CLOSE CANONGATE

BULL'S CLOSE CANONGATE

REID'S CLOSE CANONGATE

VALLENCE'S ENTRY CANONGATE

NORTH SIDE OF CANONGATE FROM JEFFREY STREET

MID COMMON CLOSE CANONGATE

OLD TOLBOOTH WYND CANONGATE

DUNBAR'S CLOSE CANONGATE

PANMURE CLOSE CANONGATE

BROWN'S CLOSE CANONGATE

LOCHEND CLOSE CANONGATE

GLADESTONE COURT CANONGATE

REID'S COURT CANONGATE

CAMPBELL'S CLOSE CANONGATE

FORSYTH'S CLOSE CANONGATE

GALLOWAY'S ENTRY CANONGATE

WHITEHORSE CLOSE CANONGATE

THE WHITE HORSE INN FORMALLY BOYD'S INN AND THE COACH AND HORSES.

The coaches left from Boyd's Inn of St Mary's Wynd, known as The White Horse Inn, for London. The White Horse Inn was also the main dropping off point for the coaches from London which was in Boyd's Close off Boyd's Entry at the back of the present day White Horse Inn, Canongate. The White Horse Inn was also the place that runaway couples from England came to be married and many weddings were carried out there. The White Horse Inn consisted of a house for entertainment, stables for over 100 horses and sheds for over 20 carriages and rooms for the guests. This was the first 5 star lodging in Edinburgh the proprietor being James Boyd. James Boyd Sold the White Horse Inn in 1776 to retire.

Samuel Johnson was known as the most distinguished man of letters in English history. He befriended James Boswell in London and travelled to Edinburgh with him prior to touring Scotland together. James Boswell lived in James Court and often took the important travellers of the time home with him. The inscription below can be seen on the wall at Boyd's Entry off St Mary's Street Edinburgh.

WHO FIRST CHARGED FOR LUGGAGE WHEN TRAVELLING?

FIRST COACH TRIPS BETWEEN SCOTLAND AND ENGLAND MANY SIMILARITIES TO TODAY'S AIRLINES.

The first stagecoach starting from the Canongate and ending in London was on October of 1712. Starting at the Coach and Horses later to be Boyd's Inn and now The White Horse Inn at the top of the Canongate. Passengers would meet prior to their journey and pay the fee of £4 and 10 shillings (£4.50p) for the whole journey, allowing each person with luggage of 20 pounds weight, and any additional weight would be charged at 6d (2.5p) per pound in weight (less than 1/2 kilo). The coach left at 6 in the morning and took a total of 13 days subject to no accidents or mishaps and no overnight stops.

MOROCCO LAND

LOOK UP HIGH ON THE BUILDING ACROSS THE ROAD FROM THE WHITEHORSE INN TO FIND

MOROCCO LAND CANONGATE EDINBURGH

The sculpture of a Moor faces forward with arms down at his sides supporting a blank shield. The sculpture was moved from its original position on an adjoining building when the present building was being redeveloped. The story of how the land (building) was named is that a young man Andrew Grey, an Edinburgh resident, was sentenced to death for rioting. He fled to Morocco and after a number of years made his fortune and returned home and was involved in saving the life of the daughter of the Provost who was perilously ill with the plague (presumably for this his sentence was commuted). He ended up marrying her and they made their home in the building where the little statue was erected.

This came to be known to the locals as "Morocco Land".

CHESSEL'S COURT CANONGATE EDINBURGH

CHESSEL'S COURT was built in 1748 as mansion apartments for the architect Archibald Chessel and in 1769 became the Excise Office and was the scene of an armed robbery in 1788 by the notorious William Deacon Brodie and his gang. The robbery failed and Deacon Brodie was eventually caught and executed on the gallows in the High Street that he designed.

OLD PLAYHOUSE CLOSE was entrance to the Playhouse Theatre where famous actors, actresses, singers and performers would ply their trade from 1747 – 1767. The tragedy DOUGLAS was first performed here in 1756 written by John Home minister and playwright.

REID'S COURT & CANONGATE MANSE

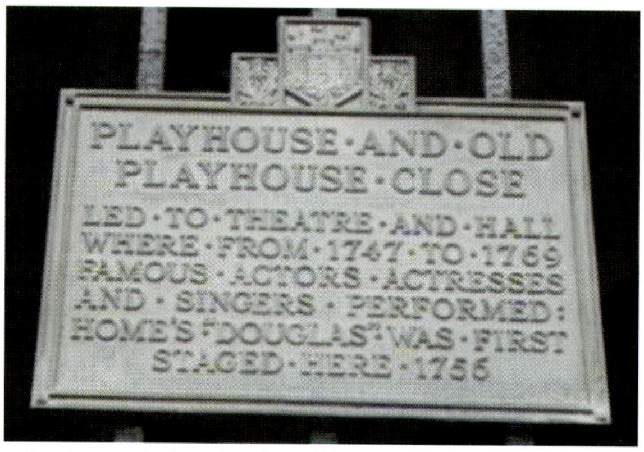

REID'S COURT takes its name from Edinburgh brewer and magistrate Andrew Reid who lived here in the 1770s. The house was first the home to Lord Advocate Sir John Nisbet and was built in 1624. It is now the Manse where the minister of the Canongate Kirk lives.

ST. JOHN'S CROSS
The cross of St John marks the spot on the Royal Mile where the boundary between Edinburgh and the Burgh of the Canongate and also marks where the original St. John's Cross was positioned.

THE OLD MORAY HOUSE was built in the early 1600s. It is now a group of three buildings and a courtyard. The Regent's House to the east was built before the mid-1600s and the new house to the south was built in 1755. Take a walk through the gates to see the buildings. The Moray House College has been on this site since 1848 and became Moray House College of Education in 1959. After merging with other colleges it is now part of the University of Edinburgh.

MASONIC EDINBURGH

SIR GODFREY HILTON THOMSON

An educational psychologist and the director of studies at Moray House College for 26 years and a pioneer of educational testing (Plaque below).

ST JOHN'S PEND

The Knights of St John had their houses in this area. Go through the Archway and you will find the Masonic Lodge Canongate Kilwinning No 2 and the oldest masonic chapel in the world.

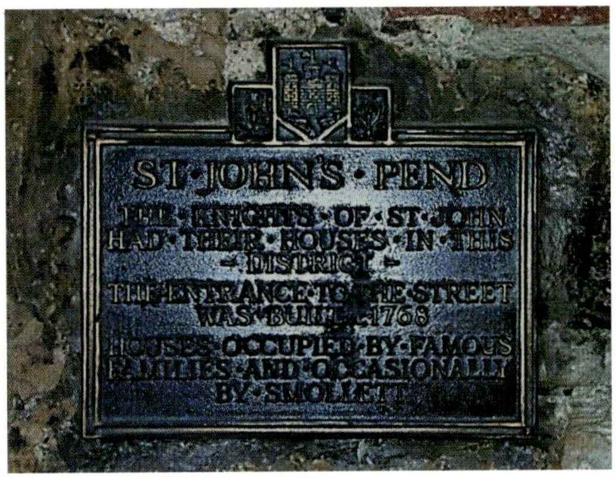

The archway below the Moray House tablet in St John's Street was also known as St John's Pend this is where the first known masonic lodge was sited, date unknown. There are other Lodges that also claim to be the first lodge by way of minutes of meetings, but St John's name has been synonymous with this area since the early 1500s. It is believed that the name was first used by the Knights of St John of Jerusalem who held property in this area. The entrance to the street that gave access to the Canongate was built in 1768 and the houses were occupied by famous families.

The Lodge Canongate, Kilwinning has had many famous brothers, Robert Burns the Poet and John Napier the inventor of the logarithms. At the first gate on the right entering from the Canongate, above a black door on the lintel, can be seen the words SAINT JOHN'S LODGE.

The next building is Lodge Kilwinning No 2 this is named after the original lodge in Ayrshire which dates back to the building of Kilwinning Abbey in 1140, however the Abbey of Holyrood built in 1124, was also linked to the freemasons and is older. The difference is, Lodge Mother Kilwinning in Ayrshire issued charters and warrants to Lodges wishing the privileges of freemasonry. In the High Street Hyndford's Close (St David's Lodge) is where Sir Walter Scott became a mason.

ST JOHN'S LODGE

CANONGATE KILWINNING No.2

HQ GRAND LODGE OF SCOTLAND

The first Lodge to request a charter was the Lodge Canongate. This was granted in December 1677 and is the first known example in the world of a Lodge being granted a Charter by an existing Lodge. The Chapel of St John is the oldest purpose built masonic meeting room in the world. The first Grand Lodge of Scotland was Lodge Canongate Kilwinning in 1735. The Head Office of the Grand Lodge of Scotland is at 96 George Street Edinburgh.

The Lodge of Edinburgh (St Mary's Chapel) No 1 has the oldest recorded meeting minutes dating back to 1598 and is still in existence in Hill Street Edinburgh today.

BIBLE LAND & SHOEMAKERS' HALL (1677). The name of the land (building) on the Canongate which has the sculpture of an open book above the front door contains part of Psalm 133 "Behold how good a thing it is and how becoming well together such as brethren are In unity to dwell". Below this there is also the following text "It is an honour for men to cease from strife". Shoemakers' Hall is an old house four stories high in which the shoemakers used to hold their meetings. Over the entrance door is the shoemakers' arms cut in stone and the figures 1667 inscribed.

CANONGATE TOLBOOTH

PEOPLE'S STORY MUSEUM

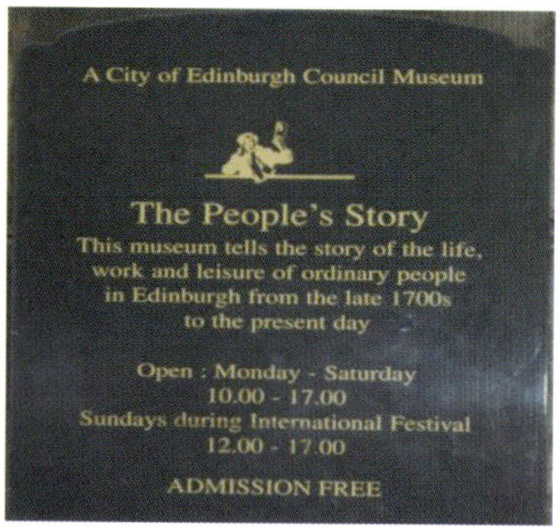

CANONGATE TOLBOOTH

TOLBOOTH CANONGATE EDINBURGH The late 15th century building is known simply as the Tolbooth. It served only the Burgh of Canongate. The Tolbooth was the town's jail. The western part of the Royal Mile the High Street was in Edinburgh and had its own Tolbooth which is no longer there. Its place is marked by the Heart of Midlothian. The Canongate Tolbooth is now home to The People's Story, a community museum, telling the story all about the people who have lived in Edinburgh from its beginning. You can find a Tolbooth in most towns to this day but none are used as jails.

HUNTLY HOUSE

THE MUSEUM OF EDINBURGH

You will find the Museum of Edinburgh in the Canongate. Inside the museum tells the story of Edinburgh from prehistoric times to the present day. Displays illustrate life in the Old and New Towns from the 1760s. Home to important collections of Edinburgh history, exhibits include Greyfriar's Bobby's collar, the National Covenant signed in 1638, and Scottish pottery. In 1825 in the 'Traditions of Edinburgh' Robert Chambers calls Huntly House the 'SPEAKING HOUSE' because of the Latin inscriptions on the building's exterior walls. There are five inscriptions, the original four inscriptions are from the 16th century and one added on renovation in the late 1920s early 1930s. The museum was housed in Huntly House (left) before an extension was built where the entrance is now. The Building was originally the Marquis of Huntly's House. Take a walk round and see the Scottish silver, pictures of old Edinburgh and maps of the building of the New Town. Free entry.

THE FIVE INSCRIPTIONS ON THE WALLS OF HUNTLY HOUSE IN THE CANONGATE

AS THOU ART MASTER OF MY TONGUE, SO I AM MASTER OF MY EARS.

MORTAL AFFAIRS ARE A SHADOW TO A STEADFAST HEART

TODAY FOR ME TOMORROW FOR YOU

I AM OLD BUT RENEW MY YOUTH.

THERE IS ANOTHER HOPE OF LIFE.

ENTRANCE TO HUNTLY HOUSE / MUSEUM OF EDINBURGH

EXTENSION NEXT TO THE ORIGINAL SPEAKING HOUSE

CANONGATE MERCAT CROSS

CANONGATE KIRK

CANONGATE MERCAT CROSS

The Mercat Cross originally stood in the middle of the road outside the Tolbooth and was moved next to the Tolbooth in the 1730s to make way for the increasing traffic. The Mercat Cross was moved to its present location in the early 1950s. Every town (Burgh) in Scotland had a mercat cross, which would stand in the middle of a market square and on occasion be the place people would be chain for a crime and have rotten fruit and vegetables thrown at them by passers-by.

CANONGATE KIRK opened in 1691.

This 17th century church designed by James Smith is unique among Scottish churches of this period. Buried in the churchyard are several famous Scots including the economist Adam Smith.

The Queen, when in residence at The Palace of Holyrood House, will use this as her local place to worship. Princess Anne's Daughter (Zara Philips) married England rugby union captain Mike Tindal here in June 2011.

ROBERT FERGUSSON was the inspiration to Robert Burns to make him the poet he turned out to be. Robert Fergusson died at the age of 24 in 1774. Robert Burns, to show how much respect he had for his fellow artist, paid for his headstone and wrote his inscription.

No sculptur'd marble here, nor pompus lay,
No story'd urn nor animated bust;
This simple stone directs pale Scotia's way
To pour her sorrows o'er her poet's dust.

ROBERT FERGUSSON

CANONGATE KIRK GRAVEYARD

1 ADAM SMITH GRAVE

2 DAVID RICCIO

4 SIR WILLIAM FETTES

FETTES COLLEGE

DAVID RIZZIO 1533 – 1566 Mary Queen of Scots' private secretary and confidante, David Rizzio, was assassinated in the Palace of Holyrood House by Mary's husband, Lord Darnley and a group of his allies on the 9th March 1566. This was his first steps to take over and rule as King. It was a short power struggle as Lord Darnley was murdered on the 10th February 1567, less than one year later. David Rizzio was of Italian descent from near Turin and was known as David Rizzio, David Riccio or David Rizzo.

ROBERT FERGUSSON'S GRAVE

5 ROBERT FERGUSSON

3 (CLARINDA) AGNES MACALEES ROBERT BURNS ONE TRUE LOVE

ROBERT ADAM PAVING STONE OUTSIDE GATES

FAMOUS FIVE. Among the people who are interned in the Canongate graveyard are **Robert Adam** Economist and author of The Wealth of Nations, **Sir William Fettes** Lord Provost of Edinburgh, Tea and Wine Merchant and funder of Fettes College, **Agnes MacAlees** (**CLARINDA**) Robert Burns one true love - the love affair was to last until their death, **David Rizzio** Mary Queen of Scots private secretary and **Robert Fergusson** Royal Poet and inspiration to Robert Burns.

DUNBAR'S CLOSE AND GARDENS

DUNBAR'S CLOSE named after the owner of the tenement at that time, an Edinburgh lawyer David Dunbar. Take a walk through Dunbar's Close for a look at a 17th century style garden with views of Calton hill, the Nelson Monument and Burns memorial in the background. On your right of the gates as you enter are Caddell House and Panmure House, the later is where Adam Smith lived and died (1772-1790).

PANMURE CLOSE / PANMURE HOUSE

Panmure House, is where the Jacobite Earl of Panmure had his town house and later Adam Smith lived and died (1772-1790). Adam Smith is buried in the Canongate Kirk Graveyard and his statue is in the High Street near St Giles Cathedral. The poppies on the gates were to show that this was the access to the Lady Haig Poppy factory between 1931 – 1965.

SCOTTISH POETRY LIBRARY

The Scottish Poetry Library can be found in Crichton's Close in the Canongate. One of only three Poetry Libraries in the United Kingdom. The Library has the largest collection of Poems in Scotland and if you are looking for the poem for a loved one or special occasion, you will find it here. There is a shop. Entry and use of the Poetry Library is Free. So do not go past go in and find the poem for you.

GOLFER'S LAND is a tenement building purchased with winnings from a 4 ball golf match between Baillie John Paterson and The Duke of York (King James VII) and two English noblemen.

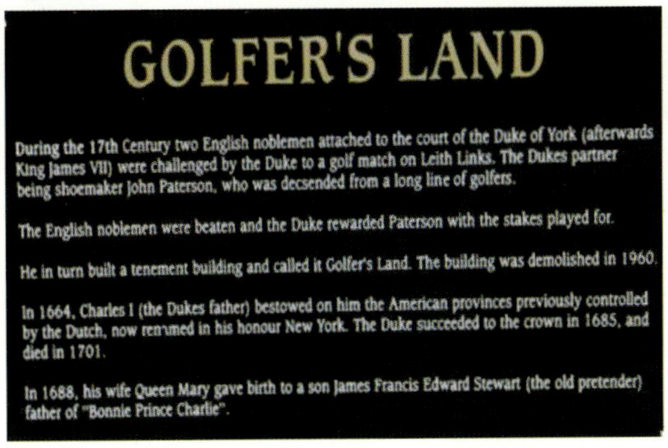

GOLFER'S LAND

During the 17th Century two English noblemen attached to the court of the Duke of York (afterwards King James VII) were challenged by the Duke to a golf match on Leith Links. The Dukes partner being shoemaker John Paterson, who was decsended from a long line of golfers.

The English noblemen were beaten and the Duke rewarded Paterson with the stakes played for.

He in turn built a tenement building and called it Golfer's Land. The building was demolished in 1960.

In 1664, Charles I (the Dukes father) bestowed on him the American provinces previously controlled by the Dutch, now renamed in his honour New York. The Duke succeeded to the crown in 1685, and died in 1701.

In 1688, his wife Queen Mary gave birth to a son James Francis Edward Stewart (the old pretender) father of "Bonnie Prince Charlie".

During the 1600s two English noblemen attached to the court of the Duke of York (to be King James VII) were challenged by the Duke to a golf match on Leith Links. The Duke's partner was shoemaker John Paterson a descendent from a long line of golfers. The English noblemen were beaten and the Duke rewarded Paterson with the stakes that had been played for, which enabled Paterson to build a tenement building which he called Golfer's Land. The building is no longer on the site as it was demolished in 1960. In 1664 Charles I (The Duke's father) bestowed on the Duke of York the American provinces previously controlled by the Dutch now renamed in his honour, New York. The Duke succeeded to the crown in 1685, and died in 1701. In 1688, his wife Queen Mary gave birth to a son who was later to be father to Bonnie Prince Charlie.

PAX **(PEACE)** INTRATIBUS **(ENTERED)**
SALUS **(SALVATION)** EXEUNTIBUS **(DEPARTING)**

NISI DOMINS FRUSTRA
EXCEPT THE LORD IN VAIN

(INSCRIPTION TRANSLATION ABOVE).

82 - 84 Canongate was Nisbet of Dirleton's House. The house with shop was originally built in 1624 by Lord Dirleton, Sir John Nisbet the Lord Advocate. This is one of the oldest surviving houses in the Canongate.

JENNY HA'S CHANGE HOUSE 1600-1857

JENNY HA'S CHANGE HOUSE (TAVERN)
On this site stood a well known tavern which was the rendezvous of poets Gay and Allan Ramsay and other renowned figures of the period. The plaque can be found on the side of the building outside Whiteford House.

WHITEFORD HOUSE Earl of Winton's' town mansion, better known as Lord Seytoun's lodging in the Canongate. In front of the mansion, in which Sir Walter Scott lays some of the scenes of the "Abbot". There was a tavern built chiefly of lath and plaster, known as "Jenny Ha's". The landlady was famous for her claret. Gay, the poet, is said to have frequented the tavern during his short stay in Edinburgh. It was a custom for the merchants and distinguished gentlemen of Edinburgh to adjourn after dinner parties, to enjoy claret and merrymaking at Jenny Ha's.

WHITE HORSE CLOSE CANONGATE EDINBURGH

The White Horse Inn at the back of White Horse Close in the Canongate is where a plaque denotes that this was the first point when leaving by coach to London. But this may not be the correct White Horse Inn as there is a White Horse Inn at the top of the Canongate which is connected to Boyd's Close in St Mary Street or White Horse Close as it was often Called, which opens into Boyd's Entry as there had to be stables for the horses and a place for the coaches Boyd's Entry looks most likely to be the original starting point for the coach and horses. There are a number of plaques That have been put up stating this is where but in fact the plaques are in the wrong place.

WHITEHORSE CLOSE On the walls in the close look for the plaques of William Dick founder of the Edinburgh veterinary college (The Royal Dick Vet) and the Whitehorse Inn said to be the starting point of the long coach ride to London. The plaque can be found on the wall of the house at the back of the courtyard where the Inn was. This area was also used in 1745 by the officers of the Jacobite army prior to the battle of Prestonpans lead by Bonnie Prince Charlie.

THE GIRTH CROSS, like the Mercat Cross in the High Street, was a place for public proclamations, and executions. One of the most famous to take place here was that of the beautiful Jean Livingston (Lady Warriston), daughter to the Laird of Dunipace and wife of John Kincaid of Warriston. On the 2nd July 1600 she had Robert Weir, a servant of her father, batter her husband to death, an idea given to her by her nurse. Both the nurse and Lady Warriston were arrested and convicted of the murder of her husband, John Kincaid of Warriston. The nurse was burned on the Castlehill at 4 o'clock in the morning and at the same time Lady Warriston was beheaded by the "Maiden" (early type of guillotine) at the Girth Cross at the foot of the Canongate. This device, which can still be seen at the National Museum of Scotland in Chambers Street, Edinburgh, claimed over 150 victims during its period of use, including, Regent James Douglas 4th Earl of Morton, who originally introduced the "Maiden" from France. The servant Robert Weir was broken on the Breaking Wheel in 1603 for his crime (a brutal and agonising death).

WHERE THE "MAIDEN" STOOD IN THE 1600s

The Water Gate was the gated entrance to the Canongate. From outside the walls it would have stood between the Sanctuary building and what is now Russell House. The Water Gate took its name from a horse pond near to the bath house.

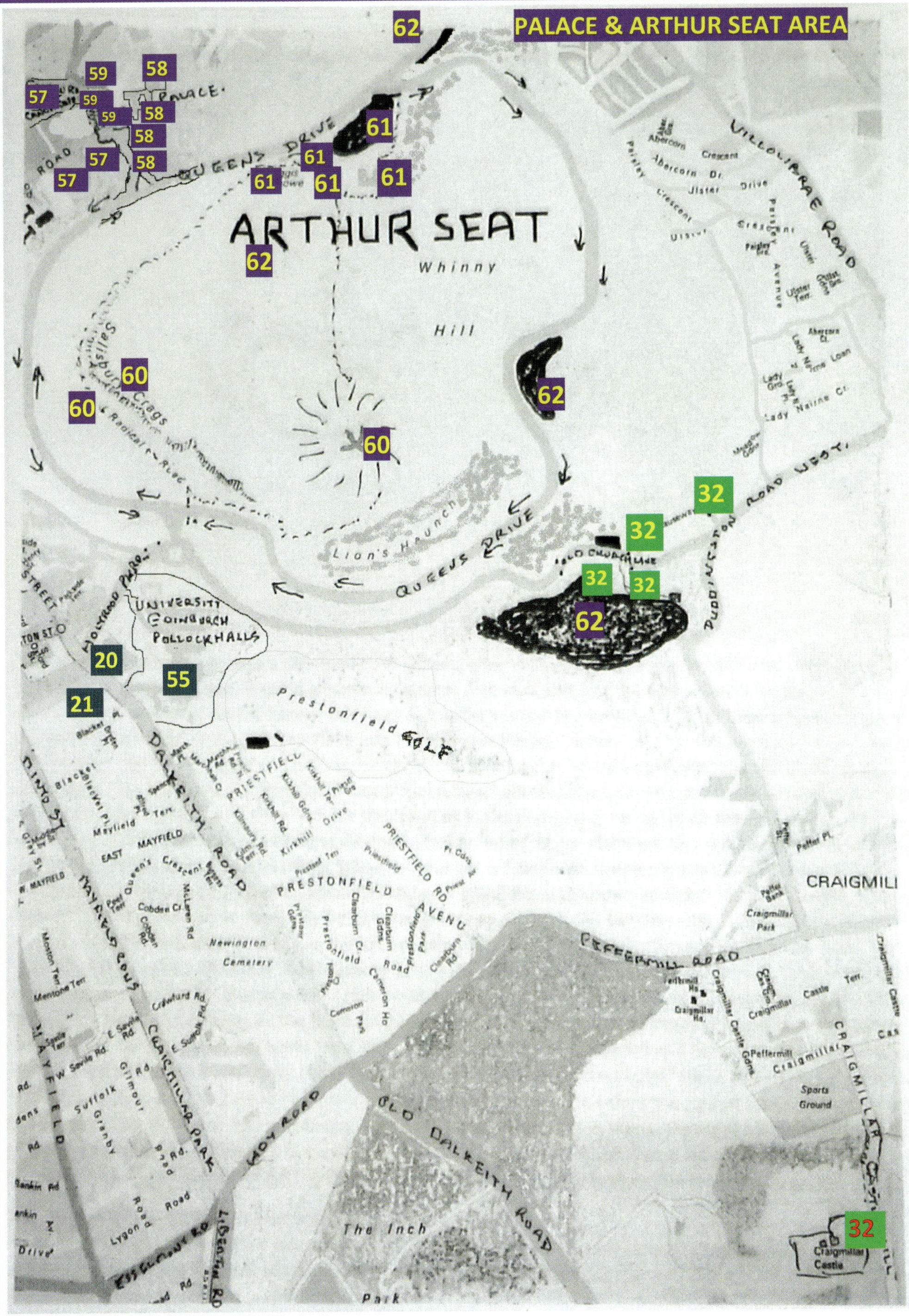

ROYAL MILE BOOK 1

57 SCOTTISH PARLIAMENT
57 OUR DYNAMIC EARTH
57 RUSSELL HOUSE

58 HOLYROOD PALACE
58 HOLYROOD ABBEY
58 QUEEN'S GALLERY
58 HORSE WYND

59 QUEEN MARY'S BATHHOUSE
59 ABBEY STRAND
59 PALACE ENTRANCE
59 SANCTUARY COBBLES
59 GIFT SHOP
59 SANCTUARY HOUSES
59 PALACE FOUNTAIN

60 ARTHUR SEAT
60 RADICAL ROAD
60 SALISBURY CRAGS

61 ST ANTHONY'S CHAPEL
61 ST ANTONY'S WELL
61 ST MARGRET'S WELL
61 ST MARGRET'S LOCH
61 FRESH WATER STREAM

62 DUDDINGSTON LOCH
62 DUNSAPIE LOCH
62 MUSCHAT'S CAIRN
62 COFFIN'S OF ARTHUR SEAT

PAGE 32 BOOK 3

32 CRAIGMILLAR CASTLE
32 HOUSE OF WAR COUNCIL
32 SHEEP HEID INN
32 LOUPIN-ON-STAIN
32 JOUGS (DUDDINGSTON KIRK)

BOOK 3 SOUTHSIDE
20 COMMONWEALTH POOL
21 SYNAGOGUE HEBREW CENTRE
55 POLLOCK HALLS

ROYAL MILE ABBEY STRAND AND HORSE WYND

THE PALACE OF HOLYROOD HOUSE ABBEY STRAND EDINBURGH

The Queen's official residence in Scotland was built in 1498 by James IV.

HORSE WYND HOLYROOD

PALACE AND ABBEY AND ARTHUR SEAT

HOLYROOD ABBEY built by King David I in 1128 is now a ruin with a history that spans 800 years. Holyrood Abbey's position close to Edinburgh Castle meant that it was often visited by Scotland's monarchs throughout the centuries.

QUEENS GALLERY

The Queens Gallery opened in 2002 to house pictures, paintings and photographs of the queen her family and her travels around the world. This building was first erected in 1840s.

HOLYROOD ABBEY

Holyrood Abbey was the site of the coronations of James II in 1437 and Charles I in 1633. It also housed the first high school of Scotland.

IR5 STANDS FOR KING JAMES THE V
THE UNICORN
BEING SYMBOL OF SCOTLAND

QUEEN MARY'S BATH HOUSE

Queen Mary's bathhouse was associated with Mary Queen of Scots.
Used as a summer house for the Royals when walking in the garden.

PALACE FOUNTAIN

The Fountain in the grounds of Holyrood House Palace.

BOUNDARY OF SANCTUARY

GIFT SHOP

Part of the original sanctuary buildings

Left of picture remaining Abbey Laird's Houses

HOLYROOD PALACE

The Palace was set alight and burned down in November of 1650 when Cromwell's troops were leaving. This was said to be an accident. The Tower of James V being the only part that survived. The present palace foundations were laid in 1671 and the rebuild completed in 1674, the new occupants took up residency at the end of 1679. The then Duke of Albany and York to be James the II of England and VII of Scotland and family.

SANCTUARY HOLYROOD ABBEY

You can find the brass S's in the cobbles of Abbey Strand leading to the entrance of Holyrood Palace. Holyrood Abbey was designated as a debtor's sanctuary in the 16th century. The sanctuary extends to the whole of Holyrood Park slightly over 4 square miles. Anyone in debt could flee their creditors, and imprisonment or hanging, by taking up residence within the sanctuary, due to this a small community grew to the west of the palace most of the houses were demolished and only a few remain. "Abbey Lairds", were only able to leave the sanctuary on Sundays as it was not allowed to arrest anyone on the Sabbath. In 1880 the law was changed which meant debtors could no longer be imprisoned. The Sanctuary building is now used as a gift shop for the palace.

THE SCOTTISH PARLIAMENT BUILDING EDINBURGH

THE PARLIAMENT ENTRANCE

The home of the Scottish Parliament sited on Horse Wynd. Construction of the building commenced in June 1999 and the Members of the Scottish Parliament held their first debate in the new building on 7 September 2004. The formal opening by Queen Elizabeth took place on 9 October 2004.
Take the free tour of the building.

OUR DYNAMIC EARTH

DYNAMIC EARTH is a science centre in Edinburgh. The centre opened in 1999. The building's structure consists of a steel mast-supported membrane stretched over a steel skeleton. Dynamic Earth takes you on a journey through our planet's past, present and future, with interactive exhibits and impressive technology, including a 4D and 3D experience. Beginning with the Big Bang, children and adults alike can witness the creation of the Earth, follow the planet through its evolution and even catch glimpses of the earth's future.

RUSSELL HOUSE CANONGATE

Russell House was named after Sir Robert Russell for all the effort he took to have the building saved for posterity. This is an example of a 17th Century tenement that the local Edinburgh people of the time would have live in. The Canongate was founded in 1140. King David I gave permission to the Canons of Holyrood Abbey to create the Burgh and it became part of Edinburgh in 1856.

ARTHUR'S SEAT in Gaelic was originally pronounced **ARD- NA –SAID.** It was a volcano that has shaped the land of Edinburgh for over 1000 years. Arthur Seat rises above the city to a height of 822 feet and provides excellent panoramic views of the city. It is a favourite place for visitors to climb as it is relatively easy to climb and is popular for hill walking. You can climb Arthur Seat from almost any direction. The easiest is from the east. Enter at Duddingston gates where there are steps for the first part then a grassy slope rises above Dunsapie Loch to the summit. The Radical Road is a footpath which will take you along the top of the slope immediately under Salisbury Crags which has long been a popular walk, giving a view over the city. It became known as the Radical Road after it was paved in the aftermath of the Radical War of 1820. There are three lochs that surround Arthur's seat, Duddingston Loch, Dunsapie Loch (where Bonnie Prince Charlie and his army rested over night prior to the battle of Prestonpans) and St Margaret's Loch, the later where you can feed the birds and Climb to St Anthony's Chapel and St Anthony's well which is said to give good fortune. Arthur's Seat also has a particular significance to the history of the Church Of The Latter-Day Saints as this is where the nation of Scotland was dedicated in 1840 for the preaching of the gospel. The apostle Orsan Pratt of the Church of Jesus Christ of Latter-day Saints (The Mormons) arrived in Scotland in early 1840 and climbed the hill to pray to god for more converts. There is a road that runs around the hill and you can see the three lochs.
St Anthony's Chapel Stands on The Fairies or Haggis Knowe overlooking St Margaret's Loch. The beacon was put at the top of the hill in 1688.

THE PATHWAY AROUND THE CRAGS AND THE PATHWAY ACROSS FROM THE CAR PARK AT HORSE WYND

Climb Edinburgh's extinct volcano. A good day out for all, with plenty to see and do, free of charge. See the whole of Edinburgh and beyond, good shoes and warm clothes required.

Away to the top and up the Crags

SALISBURY CRAGS A GREAT WALK AND A GREAT VIEW

ARTHUR SEAT

There is a road that you can cycle, walk or drive that goes around Arthur Seat, which you can access from the East side of St Margaret's Loch, which is to the left of Holyrood House Palace as you enter the Queens Park from Horse Wynd. You can also see St Margaret's Well and the steps to the start of the Radical Road across from the car park at the side of Horse Wynd. If you follow the road that passes above St Maragret's Well you will come to St Anthony's Well just down from St Anthony's Chapel, continue on and the path will take you to the top of Arthur Seat. You will not be alone as it is very popular way to the top.

ST MARGARET'S WELL

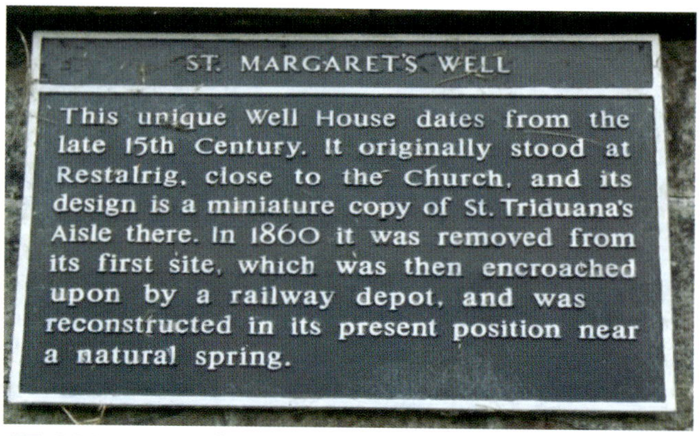

ST ANTHONY'S CHAPEL

The Chapel could have been built as early as the 14th Century, as it was reported that the Pope gave a donation for repairs in 1426.

ST MARGARET'S LOCH

Swans and Duck have been kept in the Loch since as early as the 16th Century. It was also place for boating.

THE STREAM FROM SAINT MARGARET'S WELL

ST ANTHONY'S WELL

The beginning of a fresh water stream that was said to have healing properties can be found in the hill close to St Anthony's Chapel on Arthur Seat in Edinburgh. The water once flowed from under the boulder but is now dry. A tradition in Edinburgh is on the first day in May to climb to the top of Arthur Seat and wash your face in the dew at sunrise and make a wish at St Anthony's Well. This was to give eternal beauty and to celebrate the gathering of the May Dew. The stream now flows into Saint Margaret's Loch from Saint Margaret's Well.